*Early Insights on **"Visualizing Business"***
by M. Pell

" M. Pell's ability to imagine not only the future of business, but that of humanity's interactions with technology at large, is an important perspective that we should all understand and embrace."

– Refik Anadol
Media Artist, Legend

" Mike has expertly synthesized what we have all been thinking and working towards - a new visual language for interacting with and interpreting data, powered by AI. Brilliant."

– Amy Peck
CEO, EndeavorXR

" This is a virtuosic command performance of visionary digital transformation concepts. Individually brilliant, and collectively almost overwhelming in scope and intricacy. Truly remarkable."

– David Brunner
Founder & CEO, ModuleQ

Visualizing Business

*How **Artificial Intelligence, Data Visualization,**
and **Spatial Computing** are transforming how
we see and understand global business*

M. Pell

Foreword by Refik Anadol

Afterword by David Brunner

FUTURISTIC DESIGN

Visualizing Business

Designed, written, illustrated, edited, and produced by **M. Pell**

ISBN-13: 978-1-7336870-7-2

Second Edition, September 2023
Printed in the USA

Published by

Futuristic Design, Inc.
Seattle | New York City

VisualizingBusiness.com

This one is for all of us.

CONTENTS

BOOK SUMMARY

AI is a time machine for business.

By ingeniously combining Artificial Intelligence, Data Visualization, and Spatial Computing technologies into what can be described as a "4D spreadsheet", we can finally see and deeply understand what's truly happening in businesses.

The real breakthrough enabling these futuristic business intelligence systems is the ability to manipulate time itself. By rewinding through historical data or quickly fast forwarding into the future, we have both invented and realized one of the most impactful advances in global business, ever.

BOOK FOCUS

"Visualizing Business" is an **overview** and exploration of the concepts behind an innovative new approach to seeing and understanding our businesses, referred to here as "4D".

This book is **not a blueprint** for exactly how to architect and build out next gen 4D business systems, but rather a detailed directional guide and fuel for the imagination. The book does touch on most foundational concepts and critical aspects of these systems and why they're significant.

This book is **not a deep dive** into any specific details of AI, Spatial Computing, Data Viz, or Web3 technologies. There are so many great posts and books on those topics, I'm trying to do something different – simply create an approachable, high-level, enjoyable read for anyone, not just techies.

AUTHOR'S NOTE

None of this book was written by ChatGPT.

Why? I actually like writing :-)

M. Pell

Beautifully Meaningful

by Refik Anadol

There are times when you recognize the work of kindred spirits as being so related to your own, you can immediately picture working together. It was exactly that way when I met Mike Pell for the first time many years ago in my LA studio. His understanding of what my pioneering experiments in data art could mean to the future of business was uncanny. He just got it. And in that moment, we could both see a path to combine our related visions into a single thought that could change our collective future.

This book is the start of that journey.

Mike Pell and I both share an important underlying belief that our creative ideas and experiences need to be for anyone, of any age, and any background. Even though our domains and tools are quite different, his business and mine the arts, we are deeply interested in the same question of how to represent complicated connections and networks in life through data visualization. This fundamental overlap in how we approach visualization also informs the way we view data's future role in clarifying things rather than simplifying them. We both work toward bringing data to life to convey meaning.

Building on Mike's vision for the future of data started in his last book, *The Age of Smart Information*, here he provides yet another sweeping and groundbreaking study. This time on how our businesses can be transformed by AI-generated simulations – what he terms as "4D" business systems. In this book, Pell presents an elegant, beautiful, functional, and accessible framework that shares a lot of common elements with my own artistic vision of making the invisible visible through AI-based immersive art.

Several of the topics Mike discusses here are very close to my own heart and evident in my work. Creatively using technology to uncover some very fundamental but overlooked aspects and patterns within data sets is central to my approach. He does it for business-related or workplace interactions with the help of AI, while I use AI to reveal the underlying beauty and wonder of vast data sets in unseen ways.

Another important aspect that we share in our thinking process is an emphasis on finding a people-centric method to the madness of dealing with continuous change and evolution. Innovation for innovation's sake is never part of the conversation. Pell describes this in detail to make the point that our goal is the same – technology is a great enabler for us as people to see, understand, and revel in the wonder of our imaginations and dreams. Not to make us conform or push us into an uncomfortable race to keep up with change.

I also agree with him that embracing complexity is essential while grappling with Generative AI. He states here that "Visualizing is understanding", and I couldn't agree more. Static representations fall short of conveying the truth in a constantly evolving world, feeding on incessant data flows. We need to build strong bridges between the cold, sterile, and completely data-based analytical inquiries, and these new people-based solutions. What I try to achieve through art is what Mike Pell is trying to address through his 4D approach: putting people at the center of a world operating on machine time.

Mike writes and concludes that those who learn to use the ability to manipulate time through this new technology will gain more insight into the future, and we can only hope into themselves, as well. Over the centuries, we have always created time to reflect on art. Perhaps it's now time to reflect on the people side of our business pursuits.

As I started off saying, we share many of the same fundamental approaches in our work, such as the "upleveling of information" and "turning data into insights", but here, Pell has put together so many elements of his methodology seamlessly, it feels like his assertion that we can, on demand, "engineer a composition of multiple channels of perception and cognition" is actually easy. And we can only hope it will be for both artistic pursuits and business.

"Responsibility" is a crucial word for the author, and towards the end of the study, Pell shares a list of items that need further attention for us to build an AI-assisted future "with our ethics intact." In this regard, I think that the impact of this book will go beyond its current scope at the intersection of information science, artificial intelligence, business, and communication studies, and reach the growing field of AI ethics.

And finally, Pell's brilliant perspective on applying a multi-dimensional, cinematic approach to business communication shows how 4D is not only a powerful model, but also a beautiful visualization of our world, borrowing fundamental elements from my approach to visual storytelling and aesthetics.

This book offers a very timely discussion of the transformative potential of 4D visualization systems for business globally, but also showcases M. Pell's critical insights and perspectives accumulated through three decades of practical experience in the tech industry. His ability to imagine not only the future of business, but also that of humanity's interactions with technology at large, is an important perspective that we should all understand and embrace.

Welcome to our world of beautifully meaningful data.

Refik Anadol
Los Angeles, CA
July 2023

Refik Anadol is an internationally renowned media artist, director, and pioneer in the aesthetics of machine intelligence.

VISUALIZING BUSINESS

Beyond Office

"I, for one, welcome our new AI overlords."
– Kent Brockman

There's something so unmistakably right about real breakthroughs that we often dismiss them as simple, or self-evident. Perhaps it's the way they immediately make sense to us. Or perhaps it's the feeling that things should have always been this way. True innovations tend to be straightforward, elegant, and insightful, while showcasing flashes of pure genius. They have that endearing quality of somehow making us feel like any one of us could have come up with them. It looks so easy. I mean really – the solution was there, hiding in plain sight, all along.

You know it when you see it.
True innovation is completely obvious.

We've all had these sudden moments of realizing there's a much better way. Sometimes it's a fleeting thought, sometimes a detailed plan, but always a thrilling experience in that moment. Even though few of those big ideas ever turn out to be true innovations, they all seem clever enough for us to try out. And sometimes, mixed in among all those ingenious thoughts, are some truly world-changing concepts that somehow become real. They make us immediately think "wow, it should have always been that way". And that's the magic of real innovation.

This book "Visualizing Business" details one of those truly world-changing ideas – let's call it the "4D spreadsheet" for now. The reason we refer to this as 4D (utilizing the 4th Dimension) is that it extends the 3D world we exist in by adding the dimension of **time** to the equation. Having time at our disposal makes it possible to fast forward and rewind reality, at will, giving us control over not only examining the past but leaping into the future.

Projecting forward in business has been exceptionally hard, inaccurate, and expensive to do up until now.

This novel approach of using 4D tools to analyze and eventually run our businesses will not only let us finally *see* how they work in a highly visual, deeply interactive way, but also makes it possible to *understand* them from quite different perspectives.

Let's think about that for a moment – instead of having to figure out everything about a spreadsheet, chart, or report for yourself every time, it's now explained at the perfect level of understanding for you personally. That's a huge shift from today where we are left to figure out every detail and nuance for ourselves. (Author's sidebar: that particular aspect of transforming business communication was covered in my last book *"The Age of Smart Information"*, but this idea is even bigger than that). It also means that by using our newly found knowledge, we can play what-if endlessly to see potential results.

This concept already has all the makings of a great leap forward, and we haven't even gotten to the good part yet. 4D will enable us to examine businesses in ways we could never imagine before. By safely observing how operations are unfolding from multiple perspectives, we can see how our systems work from the most detailed level, all the way up to an abstracted overview. Add to that the ability to quickly rewind using historical data and fast forward through AI-powered projections, and we have an approach which can lead to new insights and better decision making.

We can now play out whatever new scenarios we can imagine, only limited by our own imaginations. Any and all outcomes are now possible. If that's not an example of game-changing capabilities, I don't know what is. So, back to the original premise – if this idea is so simple and so obvious, why hasn't this happened until now?

Let's dig a bit more into the genesis of this innovation so you can understand why it's way overdue, and why now is the right time to reboot how we visualize our businesses.

The Genesis

Let's set the Wayback machine to May 1999. I was living in the heart of Silicon Valley, working as a Chief Technical Officer for a VC-backed startup. One morning that Spring, I was working on ideas for a new way to convey business insights to investors. That task was a regular part of my role as we were continuously raising money.

Having worked in the game industry, the thought of using a web-based 3D game engine to power and deliver an impactful investor narrative seemed like a completely obvious choice. I knew we could both clarify and accelerate people's understanding of how the business worked by using the advanced animation and sound capabilities of a game engine as interactive 3D storytelling medium. We were already doing it in gaming.

Bolt of lightning. It was one of those rare moments of complete clarity for me. Or maybe too much coffee. Not sure all these years later, but it was a truly breakthrough idea in that moment. I could see perfectly how businesses would communicate their most essential metrics and information more clearly to investors and customers. And just like that, the ideas behind this book were formed in my home office.

As I started to work out the vision for this in more detail, a few things became clear. This capability needed to be for anyone, not just experts. And I thought it could be. But, we'd need to made it as easy as it was to create new slides from templates in PowerPoint.

And of course, being in the Valley, I had to think of a competitive differentiator. That would be the secret sauce to get this idea funded or greenlit to build. For me it was obvious – the key aspect would be the ability of this new system to surface the invisible aspects we all know to be true and depend on, but cannot ordinarily see. For example, how critical information flows through a company, or how some tasks have been assigned but aren't being completed. How certain people are collaborating on projects, and others not. Straightforward stuff.

In that moment, the deficiencies of productivity software seemed completely obvious – and my imagined solution, even more so. I just couldn't believe no one else had thought of this yet (or at least they weren't talking about it publicly yet). So, as one does, I quit my tech exec job at that VC-backed Silicon Valley startup, wrote up a detailed description of the idea in a business plan, and started creating working prototypes of this next generation of business software that I initially called "dimensional communications".

When I got the prototypes and business plan far enough along, I drove around Sand Hill Road in Menlo Park, CA (where I lived) attempting to raise seed round funds to chase this vision of what lies Beyond Office.

I was having alot of fun and things seemed to be going well until the Internet Bubble Burst in late May 1999. VC funding dried up almost overnight. Timing is everything they say, and this was about the absolute worst time to pitch a new venture you could imagine. No after no after no. It was brutal. Didn't have to be a genius to realize it was not going to happen for me back then, so I moved on and managed to accomplish a few other world-changing ideas over the years.

Fast forward to today. For some reason, 20+ years later, that idea I wrote up and prototyped in 1999 still hasn't been figured out and brought to market. Not by major companies, not even by unicorn startups. And I know why – the challenge of using dimensionality and motion to depict a business is now infinitely more complex. We live in incredibly complicated times with so many factors affecting our businesses. That said, the core solution is still applicable, and the world of business still has the same basic issues to contend with.

So, I'm thinking – let's do it now, together, for all of us.

The Idea

We all implicitly understand that any type of business is constantly in motion. Whether you are focused on sales, human resources, customer interactions, internal systems, supply chain, or marketing – it doesn't matter. All areas of business are highly dynamic, often chaotic, and perpetually changing. Yet, for centuries we've portrayed their status as frozen slices in time via static spreadsheets, charts, and graphs. For decades, these unchanging, and seemingly accurate views of the data at that time have sufficed.

But, nothing could be further from the truth.

Stationary depictions of businesses are fine for doing analysis and reporting on whatever period they were meant to represent, but they do little to create a shared understanding of how things actually work in reality. Those static representations omit how we interrelate, depend upon each other, communicate, and a thousand other things.

We not only need to see, understand, and analyze our organizations as they truly are (constantly in motion, changing over time, and reacting to the world around them), but we should also be able to rewind them, replay scenarios, and simulate what could happen in the future. Doing so enables us to manage more effectively and efficiently, making those key decisions by having seen their consequences in advance (thanks to some clear visualizations and simulations). Super bonus if we can do it all on-demand and in real-time.

So, let's do it.

The Journey

With all of that as the setup, I hope you enjoy how this book will take you on a journey from that original idea back in the late 1990's all the way up to synthesizing the first generation of these "4D spreadsheets".

We'll dig into how 4D will light up business process, operations, and communication in a very new way, and act as the catalyst to ignite an epic transformation of how we run our organizations. You may not have realized you were part of this journey when you picked up this book, but thanks for choosing to be here for this giant leap forward in our collective ability to understand, communicate, and simulate our businesses.

From now on, our expectation should be that everything associated with today's businesses will be visualized as a dynamic network of living, breathing, immersive systems, that depict their ever-changing nature. We'll edit and remix these depictions and simulations in any way imaginable. Our collective job will be to bring this new mindshift and approach to Visualizing Business to life, for everyone, together.

The future waits for no one.
Let's get started!

M. Pell
New York City
May 2023

PART 1

A NEW LIGHT

VISUALIZING BUSINESS

Visualizing Business

Too many key aspects of our businesses are still hidden

Q: Do you understand what's happening in your business?
A: Yes, of course.

Really?

I realize most of us would probably answer yes, even though that can't possibly be true. Why? Because in any business, of any size, anywhere in the world, there are **critical elements** that just cannot be seen. And in many cases, those hidden aspects tend to be some of the most important indicators of how things are actually going. We all know of their existence, but they don't appear on our standard reports, dashboards, or charts. We talk about them, act upon them, and even debate them – yet they stay hidden, just beneath the surface.

In fact, I'd go even further and argue these invisible elements are almost always **the most important aspects** of business, but they're not what you'd think. They have little to do with the common KPIs and metrics we all must answer for each quarter. These invisible indicators of a well-run business are primarily **people-based** aspects, including employee engagement, innovation programs, information flow, active collaborations, operational complexity, project velocity, and wellness, just to name a few. Not as cut and dry as other standard business measures like revenue, expenses, headcount, and growth – but just as important.

Today, these hidden indicators aren't represented properly within the mountains of numbers and charts we use to divine the state of the enterprise. Instead, we continue utilizing our sacred KPIs to measure the easily captured vanity metrics that boost sales and morale, or quantitative reporting to assign blame. And yet, it begs the question – if we know all this, why are we continuing on this way?

That's an easy question to answer – it's basic human nature to not want to change unless it's absolutely necessary. We all have enough problems to tackle without having to learn an entirely new way to do things, no matter how familiar and natural it may feel. And to be fair, it's really no mystery as to why all of those invisible aspects have been missing from our dashboards and detailed reports for so long – they are not completely data-based, but rather **people-based**.

Each of these people-related metrics is a bit squishier and harder to measure than the last. And they don't seem to have a quantitative grounding like traditional reporting. Yet, they are critically important parts of business, constantly shifting and evolving, and often requiring real effort to grasp the significance of. So, it does make sense (given all that complexity) we just never found an easy way to depict and grasp these highly dynamic and ever-changing areas.

Until now.

Surfacing the Invisible

Data is not a silver bullet. Just the converse. It creates a false sense of security. We've all had access to tons of data and reporting over the years. We ran our teams based on it, made key decisions on it, and plotted our next moves. Yet, most of the data we use every single day presents an incomplete or biased picture of what's really happening out there. We do make it work, but the reality of the situation is hidden in the unseen, not the reported.

In this age of accelerated innovation and ingenious hacks, you'd think getting closer to a more informed read on things should be much easier. And it is. By applying some newer technologies to data through AI, we can reveal what we could all sense, but not see – the truth of the whole organization's state, in the clearest possible terms. And with that, being able to see the reality of our ventures should become the new expectation and standard, not the exception.

Through the widespread use of Generative AI services such as Microsoft Copilot for meeting and document analysis, we can already see the start of surfacing invisible elements and their associated insights to gain a deeper understanding of the data, act more quickly on it, and foster better decision making going forward.

By utilizing a unique combination of Artificial Intelligence (AI), Advanced Data Visualization techniques, and Spatial Computing technologies, we can depict the invisible, people-related, aspects we've been discussing to go well beyond what our reports, charts, and presentations currently provide.

This book, *Visualizing Business*, is about that journey of getting a better grasp of what's happening all around us, in a highly visual way. Because we are predominantly visual creatures, hardwired to react to movement we sense, this approach feels natural and familiar. We already recognize the language of motion and its associated meanings. By leveraging that innate ability of movement to depict and illuminate our business activities, we leverage something that's been possible but missed for too long. We've already seen it in flashes when harnessing this power in animated infographics or custom digital pieces. It just hasn't made its way into the mainstream or our daily work.

Given the speed at which Generative AI has already transformed giant swaths of global practices, widespread use of next gen business visualization and AI-informed decision making seems more plausible than ever. Why? Because that combination of Artificial Intelligence and Data Visualization delivers something we all need but didn't realize was possible – an easy way to see what's actually happening, in stunning clarity.

This AI-powered approach to visualizing data is called "4D" (short for Four Dimensional) throughout the book. It primarily uses motion, time, data viz, and artificial intelligence as its foundational units to effectively reveal hidden aspects and illuminate insights. This is how we'll unlock the next generation of data-informed decision making and decisive action. But, first things first, we need to get to the heart of how all this technology can help us.

Illuminating Insights

The value of data is only as good as the people interpreting it. Data is just data – it's not knowledge. That upleveling of information comes from turning data into **insights**, which is the truly useful piece (but very hard to come by). That's where Generative AI steps in. Its ability to quickly analyze, summarize, and clearly describe the key points of documents, spreadsheets, graphs, videos, and talks has changed how we all are doing our jobs. And it will continuously improve.

Tools like OpenAI's ChatGPT are doing work in seconds that used to take us forever to get through. We've all seen how impressive this is when first trying it out. Yet, there's so much more to come. The real innovation is when these tools fundamentally transform the way that insights are recognized, communicated, shared, and acted upon (or not, as the case may be).

By using a "4D spreadsheet", we'll be able to view and work with these auto-generated insights on topics such as how information flows, the ways people communicate, impact of cost fluctuations, or how markets are behaving. That's made possible by using Deep Learning, Machine Learning, and Generative AI to harvest insights, then funneling them to advanced data visualization and interaction engines to synthesize the immersive experiences. These new data workspaces will feel somewhat familiar but deliver an unprecedented level of clarity through what can only be considered as a new type of spatial data storytelling.

There will be several key aspects of these new worksurfaces that help reveal the hidden insights – dimensionality, time, understanding, exploration, analysis, and longitudinal study.

Dimensionality – When Apple recently introduced their first Spatial Computing device, the *Apple Vision Pro*, people finally started to realize we're ready for 3D to enter the consumer market, and maybe even the business world. What we've been doing for a very long time in VR headsets suddenly got significantly cooler with Apple's design excellence applied. This is a truly wonderful thing for the industry, as the longstanding stigma of using specialty optics to gain access to the world of immersive experience is almost gone. We can get on with the business of using dimensionality for advanced data visualization. The benefits of using 3D to visualize data in multi-dimensional ways will become apparent overnight now that it's being mainstreamed and made into super cool commercials. Thank you, Apple.

Time – The genuine breakthrough, and the foundational pillar of these 4D experiences, is the ability to manipulate time to gain insight. Being able to rewind and fast forward our view of things helps ground our understanding. That's where an innate understanding movement helps so much. We just get it. And moving through time is not quite as sci-fi as it sounds – to the contrary. From our extensive experience with streaming videos, it feels familiar and natural.

Whenever you watch a YouTube video (or any streaming video), where there's a slider control to move through the footage quickly in either direction. That's sometimes referred to as "scrubbing" video. We'll do the same with data and scenarios. And frankly, it's about *time* we got here (pun intended). Being able to quickly move back and forth through past results, comparing them to what's happening now, or even forecasting future performance will deliver a vastly different picture of the business than today's common reporting and communication practices. But more importantly, it allows us to understand and explore information in very new ways.

Understanding – Like watching a 3D animation of a running combustion engine where you see the fuel being injected, spark plugs firing, and controlled explosions driving the pistons up and down – these new 4D depictions of our businesses operating illustrate how the subsystems function and interact. These realistic animations make the highly abstract very tangible, the amorphous suddenly clear, and the mysterious completely obvious. Turns out, a moving picture isn't worth a million words, it obviates the need for them.

Exploration – Another benefit to being able to deeply engage with this type of highly dynamic business animation is that it often triggers the "moment of clarity" (where things appear to snap into place) more quickly than static snapshots of information ever could. Motion and transition used in this way are quite effective at illustrating concepts, conveying action, and making key points super obvious. The more you explore, the clearer things appear to be. Add to that the cinematic quality through these stunning visuals, and we have the perfect setup for learning through unforced means.

Analysis – The Machine Learning facet of AI has already been helping to analyze and find patterns in our mountains of data for many years. Now, it will proactively look for any trends within the invisible elements as well, surfacing them as jumping off points for important conversations and deeper investigation. We're pretty good at all this already, but modern AI and LLM models will provide a much needed boost to the horsepower and scale of analysis possible. GPT coupled with autonomous agents such as *AutoGPT* can perform fairly complex analysis and tasks without the need for much if any human assistance. The possibilities are boggling for doing autonomously running, in-depth, longitudinal research and analysis.

Longitudinal Study – Using a different lens to help analyze how operations and growth have unfolded over time will assist us in truly understanding what's happened and how to be more prepared going forward. Accurately tracing and closely observing a wide variety of business variables simultaneously through time slices reveals the ebb and flow, peaks and valleys, and unexpected occurrences in ways that static charts, graphs, and spreadsheets have never been able to. And best of all, they can all be run and analyzed over periods of time you specify. Whether done historically with existing data or projected out into the future by using simulations and projection, we can do proper studies that span a long enough phase to be significant.

What's next after we can routinely gather these insights via studies to inform our next steps and actions? The answer should be to go even further. We need our businesses to have "vision" into what's about to happen to complement our newly tuned-up operational expertise.

Vision

There isn't a day that goes by without some business leader repeating their favorite cliché about the need to know what comes next before it happens – "seeing around corners", "reading minds", and my personal fav, "inventing the future." But, is vision really that important?

Turns out – yes, vision is critical in business.

Yes, those old sayings are all quite clever (not to mention how they help paint your very own Michael Scott as a visionary ;-), but the real reason they are so overused is they emphasize focusing on the biggest ongoing problem in global business: **knowing what the next move should be**. That's what everyone needs to address in their own way.

To do that, some of us have developed fairly standard routines to get us predictable outcomes, but for the majority, there's an element of chaos and randomness that creeps in, creating uncertainty.

More often than not, some critical new issue or daunting challenge seemingly comes out of nowhere. We all know how this goes – it's part of being in business. To the highly adaptive and flexible among us, dealing with those curveballs and changing conditions are what make the job feel rewarding and worthwhile. But for many of us, those stress-inducing moments have very real financial consequences, some can even make or break our businesses or careers. Any insights would make an enormous difference here.

As is oft cited, The Great One, Wayne Gretzky, played ice hockey with an uncanny knack for instinctually skating to where the puck was going to be, not where it currently was. That type of anticipation and vision is what separated him from other standout players of his era.

Yet, even with an abundance of vision, data and experience, we can't ever seem to know enough about anything to consistently make the right next move – i.e. skate to where the puck will be. It's a super frustrating and eternally vexing challenge because of one simple issue – at the moment, we can't actually see into the future. Or can we?

Simulated Futures

At the exponentially accelerated rate of innovation we're experiencing today (mainly due to the widespread integration of AI) we're going to need better visibility into the state of business systems, people, and environments to prepare for the future. Easier said than done, as those are some of the hardest things to divine in any size organization. Being able to accurately forecast revenue, predict market conditions, and anticipate competitive threats is hard stuff. Best guesses and informed hypotheses are the norm here, which are hardly convincing much of time, but it's the best we can do. Or is it?

What if we could magically see into the future? And what if this "magic" was more about artificial intelligence and predictive data-informed analysis, than illusion and persuasion? Well fortunately, through AI, simulation, and 4D, we have the means and opportunity to take fortunetelling and predicting the future out of the world of magic and into the realm of science.

ChatGPT has felt like magic right from the start. Type in a decent prompt and you almost immediately get back a stellar response or at least starting point for further conversation. That's all because of computer science, not techno-magic. Large Language Models (LLMs) are using well-reasoned methods to learn. Based on a gigantic initial corpus of material to train on, they continue to grow and evolve over time based on new data and interactions with people. The system gets better without us doing anything but using it. So, this isn't magic at all, but rather computer science and data science – yet it sure feels like magic to most people.

Let's go a bit further. What if there was enough of your company's historical and current business data available to an AI agent it could not only comment on what's already transpired, but also synthesize a prediction for the future based on running a number of simulations?

We can do that right now. It may still feel like a bit of a guess to some, but we'll have very informed and calculated predictions based on the ability to accurately simulate a business scenario that uses parameters you set, changing variables, and historical data references keeping it grounded. Eventually, we'll come to depend on these 4D simulations to help us run the day-to-day where they'll be normal and expected. But for now, they are indistinguishable from magic.

Playing 4D Chess

Anyone can seemingly predict the future correctly. It's just a parlor trick – simply a lucky guess based on a bit of insight and the ability to extrapolate. Impressive, but often chance has as much to do with the illusion as one's actual expertise and experience.

The difference for us is that we've developed incredibly clever AI systems and techniques for taking any amount of historical data as input to forecast and model future behaviors and outcomes. The underlying foundational AI models are trained on megasets of data, so we're approximating and simulating events in a realistic way. And even better results occur when it's our own data being compared and contrasted with similar companies over time. Add in current market conditions and historical customer behavior, and we have not only "vision" but ability to extend the scenario to see how things could play out over time. We are in essence playing the mythical "4D chess" match with any opponent imaginable.

AI enables the ultimate "What-if?" machine.

For decades, highly-paid consultants were tasked with the job of modeling and playing out what-if scenarios using advanced financial models. It was a highly specialized manual activity that cost a ton of time and money. That same ability to create what-if scenarios for management teams to evaluate possible outcomes is now possible on-demand, in a matter of seconds, using Generative AI systems. Talk about disruption.

Being able to play "what-if" with absolutely any part of business operations or people concerns is just one of the major leaps we enjoy from employing AI responsibly in our businesses. Reviewing what *could* happen next will be as natural as skipping ahead to see what does happen next in a streamed movie on Netflix. This is the power of basing our interaction model on time. We'll dig into this in detail next chapter.

Summary

We are entering a new era of business where people can make sense of complex situations more easily and be better equipped to make informed decisions.

Accelerating Time

Introducing "4D" – a Time Machine for Business

Just as real-time 3D graphics, higher bandwidth, and community very quickly transformed **gaming** into the highly engaging experience it is today, an equally transformative approach to communicating what's happening in **business** is now here, and rapidly taking hold.

AI-powered services and processes are quickly being integrated within the next wave of productivity tools that will greatly influence how we arrive at various decisions. As part of that, a fundamental element of business that's been missing from our toolsets far too long is about to be introduced as an accelerant and key differentiator – **time**. By adding time to the equation, we can analyze our businesses in an entirely new way – by visualizing effects over time.

4D = Space + Time + Data

This innovative approach to visualization "4D" (four dimensional) adds time to the spatial aspects of 3D. Best described as the difference between a photo and a streaming video, anything 4D is delivered with the built-in ability to rewind and fast forward through time and space, not just capture a single moment. That unique power of 4D to bring clarity by shuttling back and forth becomes evident very quickly upon first use. No longer relegated to using static snapshots in time to make our key decisions, we can now look back through any part of historical data, watching changes happen as we go, piquing our curiosity while simultaneously triggering pattern recognition. We can just as easily fast forward into the future via AI-powered projections and simulation to see many potential outcomes projected.

Simply put, we now have a **Time Machine for Business**.

The implications of this innovation are truly profound. 4D will be as transformational for business as digital spreadsheets were when they replaced the paper ledger. It's that big. Why? In the most classic of pop business terms, 4D fills a need we had that seemed too hard to address in the past – seeing into the future. It's one we were almost oblivious to given its ridiculous premise and the complexity and speed of our business operations.

The ability for 4D systems to rewind and fast forward through business operations over time ranks among the most significant advances in running and understanding our organizations – ever.

In the past, we typically made our daily operational and strategic decisions by analyzing and discussing any relevant data prepared as reports, spreadsheets, charts, videos, etc. These representations of a particular period were useful but outdated the moment we read them. Yes, we took what we had and used it to great success sometimes, and certainly utilized real-time data when it was available, but that was rare. We were continuously needing to do our own projections, while spotting patterns, and relying on our experience and intelligence as a guide, because the systems just didn't provide much more. It worked fine for decades and decades. But now, there's a better way.

Time Machine

By design, 4D constructs give us a way to clearly see our businesses at any point in the timeline – past, present, future, or even all at once. By using historical data and future simulations, we can now see how scenarios unfold over time. That provides the missing perspective we need in our reporting and analytics to further ground decisions. No matter how simple or complex, we'll develop a foundational baseline of well-understood, visually compelling, time-based representations of common scenarios – much like the standard tables, charts, and graphs which serve us today. They will feel familiar yet excitingly new at the same time, and enable a much deeper exploration at any time.

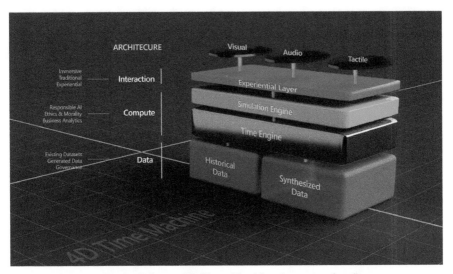

Architecture for building a 4D Time Machine to power business

For example, let's compare how we'd present the results of a new product rollout to our team using standard practices vs. a more 4D approach. Currently, when presented with a report, chart, or video to explain the actuals during a meeting, each participant needs to use their imagination to create their own mental model to help interpret what's being communicated. We don't consciously think about it per se, as it's a very necessary and common thing to do, which happens all the time as we work. Nothing new there. That said, it's a problem.

In this scenario, like many others, we're doing this mental model creation and alignment repeatedly as the actuals are worked through. And chances are, my mental model for what's happened and your mental model for the same events will look nothing like each other – never mind behaving in the same way. This cognitive mismatch often leads to confusion, mistakes, and miscommunication. It's one of the fundamental problems keeping our organizations from seizing new opportunities, or just operating efficiently.

Contrast all that to using a 4D approach, where the presenter and participants can all see and experience the actuals in the same spatial way, through an animated visualization that conveys the key points. It aligns everyone's mental models from the start and gives us a common baseline to work with that may be traditional 2D, 3D, or a spatially immersive 4D representation – doesn't matter, as each person can flip to the view that most suits their preferred way to be communicated to.

Another exceptionally useful feature is enabling any person or autonomous agent to explore the model in their own way to gain additional understanding or play what-if without affecting the view of others. They can then share edits back into the original for their team.

That's the power of having your own time machine.

Rewinding History

Going back through historical data is done all the time in business, but not in an efficient way. Before GPT-4 and advanced AI models, it was a highly manual process to gather, compare, and analyze any amount of historical data. And you could forget about wanting to see it play out over time, as that was a very specialized, expensive bit of custom business analytics work.

Now compare that with what we can accomplish in seconds using ChatGPT or similar. It's crazy. Who would have thought? And to take things even further, imagine having your very own 4D spreadsheet to fluidly scrub back and forth through historical data with any number of dimensions and variables overlayed or filtered out. It's just like rewinding back to a prior scene in a streaming movie you're watching. The power of randomly accessing specific times, days or time periods via a familiar interaction model (such as a movie player's slider) is the most natural and powerful way we've ever had to explore past events in context.

And yes I agree, rewinding through our historical business data is a relatively straightforward task – that's why we have been able to do it for awhile within some business analytics packages and investment sites, usually through a 2D slider or data blade. The part that's been missing up to now is making this easier by employing AI to scour the data graphs for us to make it easier to wrangle any kind of data, not just financial. By running deep learning and semantic algorithms over any size datasets, AI can spot and surface connections, trends, and correlations we'd never see as easily.

For example, seeing and exploring people-related scenarios such as your past hiring practices, employee retention, and promotion rates would be fascinating. Triangulating historical people data along with major internal and external events creates the potential to recognize patterns and surface insights on why things played out the way they did. Not to mention what an AI analysis of the same events and data graph would yield on the behavioral side of things. It adds yet another level of impact when presenting the findings.

What if it became apparent when watching the rollout of a new product unfold that a lack of paying out shipping bonuses directly led to a mass exodus of talent? Yes, it's an easy inference to make, and we can see these things in standard charts and graphs, but the visceral effect of seeing it play out through an animated sequence is a highly effective way to convey the immediate impact. And perhaps, this becomes a new vehicle for teams to interactively discuss and debate what could prevent this from happening in the future.

Pressing Play

The same techniques and technologies we just discussed for rewinding through history are equally as valuable for observing the current state of affairs within our organizations. Many of us have a sense for what should be happening, but seeing it unfold live (or as near real-time as you get) is utterly mesmerizing, and makes it all very real, very fast.

Whether you are interested in tracking the speed and effectiveness of outbound communication in real-time, seeing active collaborations, or watching the flow of information throughout the organization – the "Play button" gives you the power to not only visualize all of this but Pause and Resume after a closer look.

I've often described this "Now Playing" view of business as if you were watching a 3D animation of a running combustion engine or a time-lapse video of people and cars moving through a busy city. The motion of objects flowing through the organization illuminates the actions and processes in ways that become immediately apparent. Just as you see a directional path to your destination in a Map application by looking at the highlighted journey line overlaid on top of a street view, "Play mode" in 4D uses various visual techniques to convey the flow and progress of running operations.

The visual impression of witnessing a well-organized business operate in real-time can perhaps be thought of as seeing a symphony orchestra performing live – elegant and moving. Whereas watching a chaotic, poorly run business may be like seeing a punk band banging out a messy set. Both instances can be exhilarating in their own way. The important part is that you are there and can experience it live.

Being able to monitor and dig into what's unfolding in our organizations while it's happening has always been a dream for managers of all levels. Seems like it should be no big deal given our dashboards and mobile apps, but the ability to see what's going on right now in a dynamic form way is a giant leap forward, and a far cry from the days of number-heavy spreadsheet reports and byzantine charts. Using 4D as a different type of lens to observe how people are working, communicating, and collaborating is a game changer.

We can finally see businesses running right before our eyes.

Fast Forwarding

Needing to know what comes next in business is not only important, it's expected. Predicting market moves or forecasting revenues has always been standard practice – it's how we telegraph intent and set expectations for ourselves, investors, and the industry.

The significant difference now is that by using 4D techniques with well-trained foundational AI models, we can not only forecast and simulate those future outcomes, but more effectively plan for them. Whether through natural language conversational interfaces or streaming video style controls, we can fast forward through time to see the numbers and vignettes play out in the proper context. Add to that the ability to run as many what-if scenario variations as we like (rather than relying strictly on rigid formulas with no context), and we can increasingly bring the future into focus.

Remember when Marty McFly had a sports almanac of past game outcomes in *Back to the Future Part II*? Well, 4D is kinda like that, but better. How can that be true? Well, we still cannot accurately predict the actual outcome of future events, but we can model and simulate as many situations as are called for. And we'll have more confidence in the predictions than ever before – mostly due to the ability to fine tune the AI models or any part of the scenario variables to account for multiple timelines.

Let's use this simple example to illustrate how profound a change this is for us. We need to provide revenue projections and guidance for our investors this quarter. Rather than strictly relying on historical data for the same period in the previous year or two and adjusting for new products and services, we can now allow the AI models to leverage other competitors' predicted offerings and anticipated changes during the same future period. The resulting forecast may not be 100% right, but it will give us such a better data-informed view of the future than we could ever hope for currently.

Making the future feel both predictable and changeable is such a groundbreaking advancement, it still sounds completely ridiculous to say out loud. But trust me, it is real and it's here. Time to go Back to the Future, whenever we want.

Summary

Moving through Time and Space to evaluate a company's performance by simply using a streaming video-style interface is game-changing for every industry, and businesses of every size.

Embracing Complexity

Let's focus on clarity, not oversimplification

Tools that promise to help us better understand our businesses and see what's truly happening have got to excel at **clarity**. They also need to be great at illustrating concepts and processes in more straightforward ways, regardless of any underlying complexity.

Despite all our attempts at automating, streamlining, innovating, and advancing technologies, business is far more complex now than in any previous time in history. And the speed of business continues to accelerate. Even in small companies, it has gotten to the point of being too much for any one person to completely understand and explain every aspect of what they do and how it works. In spite of our efforts to be more organized, we have created a mess. A new approach is needed to make sense of all this complexity in the day-to-day, so we can focus on what's needed for us to meet the challenge of tomorrow.

When thinking about how to make sense of complex situations, it is very tempting to jump straight to the idea of simplifying everything down to just a few basic elements that are key indicators. Then we could just convey the status and operations of any organization in an easy to grasp dashboard-style chart or beautifully designed report. Sounds good. Simple is always better, right? Not so fast...

The act of trying to simplify just about anything can inadvertently lead to leaving out important elements and aspects. At first, they seem to overcomplicate the message, diagram, or explanation – so we get rid of them. Good thought, but too often that leads to a reductionist exercise rather than actually helping to clarify things. Simplifying can be dangerous when it leads to thinking too much detail is unnecessary. It certainly can be, but finding a balance of high-level summary with just enough detail is what we need to target. Sometimes that will need to come through "progressive disclosure" techniques, simply meaning don't show everything all at once. It's a balance, but doable.

We need to clarify, not just simplify.

Being Clear

Many years ago, I had the opportunity to dig deeply into designing for extreme scale and complexity on a global level, which taught me alot about clarity. The challenge was to design a way for people to quickly and clearly understand critical status indicators, then confidently take action on them (or not) during high stress situations, that commonly arise while running some of the world's fastest growing datacenters.

That experience was a masterclass in how to design for clarity, but more importantly, I learned a ton about how to communicate clearly. When severe consequences could result from my work being used in critical decision making, it's serious. Dealing with that type of extreme scale and complexity is a different kind of challenge because it turns out to be counter-intuitive to solve for. Running some of the biggest services on the planet requires a massive infrastructure, which brings complicated issues – so there's absolutely no way to simplify it down just by hiding the complexity. Modern datacenters power most of our digital existence, so they are complex, and need to absorb breakdowns to keep ticking every second, every day. Failure is not an option here.

What turned out to be the most interesting aspect of all this wasn't readily apparent at first. What I discovered was that many of the prevailing thoughts in this specialized part of the design field are backwards, and it appears we've been going about all this all wrong for a very long time. While exploring the best ways for people to quickly understand, communicate, and take action on whatever is happening in specific scenarios, some important (but non-obvious) insights became quite clear.

Clarity vs. Simplicity

People want simplicity. No one has time to figure things out anymore, nor do we want to. Making complex things appear simple gives us exactly that (if done well). Designing-in a lack of complication makes whatever you're dealing with more appealing. Super bonus points if something that's made to appear simple is also clear. Think about that. Simplicity and clarity do not always go hand in hand.

Clarity is a difficult state to achieve for many of us. It requires the communicator to put a message into terms that make perfect sense for the intended audience. That's alot harder than it seems. Even a clever representation is not necessarily going to appear clear to anyone seeing it. Finding the balance between uncluttered thought and detailed information is always the goal, and a difficult one at that. A successful blending has just enough impact to create the moment of clarity. And getting to that level of clarity is as much art as it is science. It requires gracefully separating the essence from all the surrounding concepts.

Regarding the actual form simplicity takes when communicating the complex, people tend to respond more cognitively to clarity, and more emotionally to simplicity. You may say to yourself "oh, I get it" when realizing something has just become clear, versus verbalizing to someone else "that was simple!" when encountering unexpected simplicity. They are not always going to be neatly aligned in that way, but it serves as a guide for experiential designers. When constructing the methods you'll use to deliver the message within 4D systems, you will invariably recognize that information resonates with people only when its presented in the right form and at the right altitude.

When it comes to communications within our businesses, we need to re-focus on clarity, not simplicity.

Emphasizing clarity over simplicity doesn't automatically mean your content will be more streamlined. It could turn out to be super detailed. It's one of those non-intuitive things – being clear does not preclude things from being very involved and dense. In fact, a highly effective message may not be simple at all, but rather multi-layered in its approach, supported by many facts and data. The only thing that truly matters here is that the message is understandable and actionable – the main indicators of when information has been designed well.

Clarifying Complexity

We live in complicated times, and that's not going to change anytime soon. Things are rarely simple in business, even with the addition of AI. And since it's only going to continue getting more complex each day, we need to find a better way to assess where we're at, form a plan, and execute it. Throwing technology at complexity is not going to work. It's the human part of the equation we need to focus on.

Our first instinct here might be to use design or technology to superficially simplify things, trying to make it more understandable – which in reality is working against us. What's actually needed here is a path to better understanding without sacrificing the important details or our ability to recognize complexity from both a higher-level and detailed viewpoint. Tough to balance, but that's exactly what the 4D approach brings.

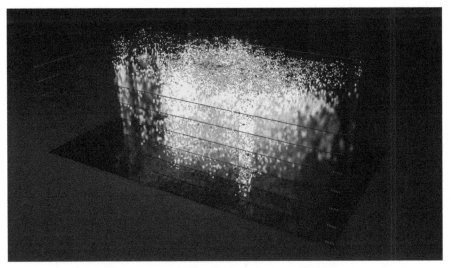

The visual intensity helps clarify the situation, not simplify the complexity
(Credit: Dave Brown, Microsoft Research)

The way we'll successfully clarify the inherent complexity in our businesses is to find the most appropriate form, medium, and delivery for the current context and at the correct altitude (meaning the right level of detail). If we're trying to get a handle on the big picture, we summarize and streamline. If we're digging into a tough decision, we see the details and reality of the situation in all its alarming glory. Need a peak at where we're headed? It's gotta be more than a few impressive looking numbers displayed using beautiful typography – we'll need to see the math on how we got there as well.

And at no point will the density of what we need to sort through be reduced to the point of obscuring the truth. You can't divide a prime number evenly with anything other than itself and one. It is what it is. Similarly, we can't consistently make better decisions without enough of the important information being available vs. hidden. You cannot simplify the complexity, just clarify it through better form. We need to embrace that.

These new AI-powered tools will become expert in visualizing our complex businesses in ways that retain the important details and data, while simultaneously appearing clear and concise. We'll know there's an easy way to get more detailed information whenever we want it, but the common views will deliver the clarity we desperately need. And not a moment too soon.

Summary

There's no way to simplify complexity without losing an essential part of the equation – detail. It's complicated.

PART 2

LEAPING
FORWARD

VISUALIZING BUSINESS

Visual Systems

Seeing is believing. Visualizing is understanding.

No question the biggest revolution in global business since the advent of the Web has been the rapid rise of Artificial Intelligence. It lets us effortlessly create, streamline, and automate business processes like never before. That said, there's something obvious missing from this global phenomenon – an equally transformative movement in business communication to complement the power of AI, based on modern visual constructs. The ability to understand business visually.

AI has fueled many leaps forward recently, including a new type of highly visual data toolset to help represent extremely dynamic, complex systems. Those visual tools could easily be considered the biggest surprise of all. Perhaps because what they enable was hiding in plain sight for so long. Or that they filled a latent need from our collective blindspot. Regardless, and as with all true innovations, this seems completely natural and obvious now that it's here. We've finally found a significantly better way to present data and information to our teams, customers, and organizations. It's 4D.

The innovative method 4D business systems use to unlock a new level of understanding is to seamlessly composite multiple channels of perception and cognition together in order to engineer the moment of clarity. These stunning visual representations are based on existing paradigms and norms, but deliver an intelligent visual representation that focuses our attention and helps surface the right information, at the right altitude. The packaging for these data visualizations were all designed to be clear and concise from the start, rather than requiring us to figure out the intended message or ourselves each and every time.

Whether we encounter dashboards, diagrams, reports, or charts, they will be capable of automatically applying an appropriate multi-dimensional visual language for data storytelling. This is a huge shift away from us figuring things out ourselves, to the data doing it for us from the start. That's going to require us to lay some groundwork in the form of standards.

4D Design Language

As with all successful leaps forward, standards must be arrived at and adopted across both our business and developer ecosystems to ensure consistent and familiar experiences while creating and consuming. For 4D systems, that requires a new visual design language to be developed to support widespread adoption with these aspects:

Accessibility	**Dimensionality**
Scale	**Dynamics**
Complexity	**Relationships**
Altitude	

These are the **foundational aspects** and principles of this new 4D visual design language. They all should be used in concert to create coherence within these systems.

Accessibility

As with many technological advancements that primarily utilize sight or dimensionality as their modality (such as spatial computing), we as an industry must carefully consider and provide more accessible forms of these experiences for people with low vision or blindness. There won't always be a perfect 1:1 alignment of the various representations (like mapping sound to visuals), but we should try harder to provide the same value and information via complementary modalities. And when combining several mediums, it's imperative for us to deliver accessible multi-channel solutions.

Audio narration, sonic landscapes, and haptic feedback provide a rich palette of alternatives to try out when augmenting visuals as the primary interaction method. We have just scratched the surface of the possibilities here – and what an exciting time to explore solutions with the help of AI and spatial computing toolkits (which will contain all of these features in the base platform over time). Designing to make those of us who are differently-abled feel like they are missing nothing is the best design outcome of all. And it's our responsibility.

Scale

The magnitude of our business endeavors is often described with the word "scale". Seems we always want to "scale up", "scale out", "scale back", and my favorite, "operate at scale". Scale is another measure of success, given its difficulty and cost.

The scale of our systems and relationships is bigger than we think

The true magnitude and scale of business is one of those critical aspects that's been hiding just below the surface for too long. We talk about it often, decide about it, and work with it – but we don't seem to actually grasp it the way you'd imagine. The numbers are always there large and bolded in some dashboard, but understanding what they truly represent to the business is quite another story.

From a human perspective, we really aren't good at understanding discrete numbers without something to directly compare them to. It's somehow assumed the big numbers alone will suffice to impress or worry us enough. And this situation often is made worse by the fact that we don't generally have meaningful enough comparisons at the ready. We need an example that can help us equate what we're presented with to something we can truly grasp and internalize. Quite simply, numbers without context lack meaning.

---

*"**Scale** can only be understood when you provide a meaningful comparison to clarify the magnitude."*

From a business perspective, I'd argue that any scale is impossible to fully appreciate without the right comparison and context. A single ominous number is just a shallow one-dimensional assertion without another object to compare to. "The scale of this project can't be underestimated" is a familiar corporate refrain, although seldom fully heeded. Too much effort is spent on presenting numbers that appear impressive or daunting versus addressing the relevant part of all this – "how does this relate to what I'm familiar with? Can I somehow put this into terms I understand and know how to take action on?".

We are all working at an almost unimaginable scale on a regular basis. Just a few years ago, even considering working at a scale of this magnitude continuously would have been a ridiculous notion. And it still is. But here we are, faced with misjudging scale every day, which tends to be extremely expensive when we get it wrong. For example, we are all guilty of not planning well enough for a "success problem" when rolling out a new service. Underestimating success (versus just problems) results in not being able to scale up fast enough to meet demand. That means unhappy customers and lost revenue.

Evaluating scale becomes even more challenging when it's used as a weapon to argue for gaining advantages such as support, budget, or corporate resources. "We'll be crushed if we don't scale out to handle this." Indeed. But that said, it does appear we are deluding ourselves into thinking we can address scale properly without having the means to evaluate the current state or the result of not scaling properly.

That's precisely where 4D visual systems shine. A big part of our efforts will be to represent scale clearly in our conversations, graphs, and reports by using a relatable **comparison** and visual reinforcement that immediately makes sense.

We know that extreme scale cannot be addressed by putting more things on the screen. That doesn't fix anything. In fact, it makes it way worse. When designing for understanding, it's always a challenging task to compare quantities or large numbers together to elicit the right response or get the relative importance across. We'll need to use compact and meaningful visual representations that leverage well understood metrics, rather than adding more objects or zeros.

Scale matters.

Complexity

Our world is inherently complex. It moves at lightspeed in some ways, glacially in others, and constantly changes in so many other ways we can't possibly keep track of. Layers and layers of stuff co-exist in a filtered, mixed, and intertwined state of being. A mind-numbing level of complexity comes with our pace of business and rate of innovation, yet we consider it so normal now we hardly give it a second thought.

As individuals, it's completely fine to focus on just the required parts of any interpersonal situation and put off any other parts before moving onto the next thing. Nothing to fret over. Just deal with the situation at hand and keep moving forward. But in business, thanks to AI, we can no longer just focus on what's right in front of our noses. We have got to develop a deeper sense of what's happening, at what pace, or be left far behind. It's that simple. And that complex.

As we discussed in the previous chapter, in many cases complexity can't be simplified. Things being complicated is a fact of life, and actually quite necessary or even unavoidable in many environments. We are fooling ourselves into thinking everything can be simplified. It can't. You simply cannot hide or obscure all the intricate workings of obtuse relationships in a global system, then expect people to fully grasp the gravity of it all before making decisions.

We do the biggest disservice to ourselves and our companies when we cloak or discard important aspects of non-trivial systems and situations. Who wants to be in the dark for the sake of being more comfortable? Conversely, this doesn't mean we should or would show every aspect of every object, person and process. But, it does mean we all need to recognize that complexity is not a bad thing, it's just a part of our world that needs to be clarified for us, so we can make better decisions and move on.

*"**Complexity** cannot be simplified, only clarified or illuminated."*

The flipside of dumbing down representations to appear simpler is putting way too much detail in. A standard approach to illustrating complex networks, systems, or relationships has historically been to try to depict and interconnect every element of a set in an effort to be precise. Good thought, but that turns out to be terrible for representing relationships between a non-trivial numbers of objects.

It would be far better to find new techniques to represent the full extent of the process, data, or network – and do it in a way that allows for a clear overview and a means to drill in. Often, we use progressive disclosure in experience design to avoid showing everything at once, then reveal what's needed when asked for. We need more of that here.

This type of balanced presentation of information, at whatever the right level of understanding (i.e. altitude) is for the given context, is where we'll start with these highly visual 4D spreadsheets. The key to doing this effectively is using layers to overlay or filter down the amount of data and information being shown at any one time.

Layers are a very common element in drawing programs where you need to stack up transparent sheets on top of one another, with each containing some part of the whole image. They're extremely useful in allowing you to isolate different elements in a separate layer. Similarly, using layers within 4D visualizations gives us complete control over what's shown and what isn't, helping to present the content clearly. Layers also become a key part of the interaction model when you can turn various overlays on and off as needed to aid further exploration and faster recognition.

Altitude

Anything can be understood more clearly if it is presented at the right altitude, or level of detail, for the person viewing it. Sometimes that's a very deep, data-laden representation. Other times, a higher-level version tends to do the trick. Regardless, finding the right altitude to reach a particular audience is what's needed for it to quickly make sense. Which level to start with won't be completely obvious in some cases, as we're all sufficiently different in our perception of concepts, but the form and representations can be normalized for each.

By dynamically morphing content's form to fit somewhere along a continuum that spans from high level summary all the way down to incredibly detailed depictions, 4D visual systems rapidly **adapt** their method of communicating to the current context. Finding which representation is most effective will depend greatly on the situation that person finds themselves in at that specific moment. Whether in the middle of a heated debate, doing a formal presentation, or just needing a summary update while on the run – current context has a real bearing on whether the message connects or not.

The ability for information to adapt itself to the current context is one of the key features of "Smart Information", which was detailed in my previous book on that subject. For example, if you are out walking with just your digital watch and earbuds, and something comes in that's normally intended as a highly visual presentation with alot of detail, the content itself will automatically figure out the correct form to utilize at that moment (which would naturally be voice-oriented).

Dynamics

The motion, behavior, and reactions of objects within these highly visual systems can be described as their **dynamics**. That refers to any additional elements applied to previously motionless forms of data or information to convey their meaning. Dynamics are what make 4D visual systems so effective in bringing insights to life – they literally make them move and react to aid in storytelling.

Motion is the most obvious and powerful addition to any type of business communication. As humans, we're hardwired to detect and react to motion of any kind. Leveraging that to track state changes and movement is how we can easily depict business processes unfolding over time. Unfortunately, we've already used motion for superfluous things like transition animations in slide decks or cute GIFs added for effect. Those have their place, but the motion we're after here shows movement and flow of frequently changing data and processes.

We need to make sure if we're using any movement, it adds value to the scenario. We'll see in the next chapter how the visual treatment of motion is critical to getting a specific meaning across. For now, consider how clear the movement over time becomes when you can visually identify the path something has taken, such as the light trails from a twirling sparkler.

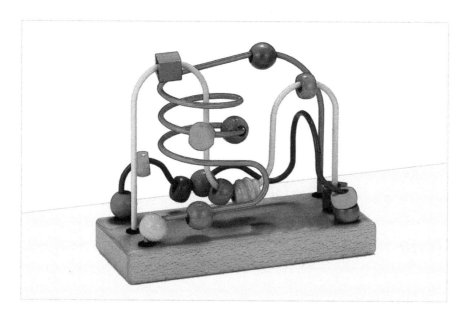

A child's toy is a great illustration of seeing the motion paths of data
(Credit: Joy Toy)

Behavior is what we expect to happen in response to stimulus. In our case, it adds natural reactions and recognizable character to any previously inanimate objects within our systems. You may wonder why adding behavior matters at all when we just talked about motion being the key to understanding. Turns out that people expect things to behave in very particular ways, whether imagined or not. Some of the best animation work done by Pixar features inanimate objects (like their signature Luxor lamp) acting very convincingly as people. If you don't think about it too hard, they are. We'll set up that same sort of expectations with data to assist us in conveying meaning through behavioral action.

Reaction is not just the response to an action. It helps define the characteristics of objects, and itself carries a significant weight and role within our highly dynamic visual systems. The way an object (or group of any kind) reacts to both stimulus or the lack of interaction is telling – and sets expectations from then on for the viewer. Knowing there's a good chance of eliciting a particular reaction as response to input gives objects and systems a sense of predictability and solidness. We'll use that to set up competitive scenarios among other things.

Together, all three of these attributes create the personality that sets 4D apart from anything that's come before. It's a system that not only aides our ability to decide and take action, but makes it feel like we are a part of the action itself.

Dimensionality

Business communications doesn't have to appear in 3D to be effective, but when used with purpose, it can make all the difference. Currently, there are few examples demonstrating how 3D is substantially better than 2D outside mapping and engineering, but when you do see an example of where this is all going it's startling. Look no further than the obvious – we all live in a 3D world, with no instruction required. We've spent our entire lives navigating our spatial landscapes and recognizing every aspect of what's found within them implicitly. It follows that some information is best delivered in a spatial way.

A favorite example of mine that illustrates the intrinsic power of dimensionality is an air traffic controller display. Tasked with closely monitoring several in-progress airplane flights concurrently, an air traffic controller will use their traditional radar display, which is of course a flat 2D circle that displays relatively crude representations of many aircraft in flight. The plane's callsign, position, altitude, and speed help to identify them on the display. Controllers need to create a mental model of where each of the flights are in relation to each other, because the 2D display has the information, but lacks the ability to delineate altitude specifically.

By flipping the current model from 2D to 3D, we give air traffic controllers the ability to leverage a combined visual and mental model vs. having to constantly recreate the relationship in their own minds. The improvement in cognition is striking. It combines two disparate concepts into one in a highly connected visual way. It's clearly an improvement. That said, we would need to preserve easy access to the traditional 2D representation to allow for quickly switching back and forth to maintain a high level of familiarity for consistency or personal preference in stressful situations.

Now let's add **immersion** to that kind of dimensionality, and we have a whole new experience when presenting data for true impact. By using affordable and widely available devices such as Virtual Reality (VR) headsets or Augmented Reality (AR) glasses, we can literally put you into the data set itself. The impact and connection when you're looking at room scale data is undeniable. There's nothing quite like looking at data in a form that resembles physical objects, such as a large sculpture in an art museum. It has volume, weight, and evokes feelings – good or bad. And while not always available now, immersion is the best way we have to make an emotional connection to the information being presented.

Relationships

The way things relate to each other is one of the most fundamental aspects of learning, about anything. And it also appears to be central to truly "getting it" when it comes to business systems. Relationships, whether you are talking about people, places, or things, need to be understood in meaningful terms to us. We draw conclusions about the importance of just about anything by its number of connections and to what or whom. As the basis of social networking, our relationships provide a logical way to consider the importance of connections between people and many other meaningful insights.

---

*"**Complicated relationships** cannot be visually expressed as a spilled box of spaghetti."*

We'll use our 4D visual language to show active relationships and convey how information is flowing between them. This will focus on the multiple layers of relationships, not just the connection points. This contrasts with the way business analytics and data visualization packages depict complex relationships today. They are generally more confusing than enlightening. Their approach to showing networks and connections has historically been to try to depict every element of a data set or collection in an effort to be precise. Good thought, but that type of overdrawn visual layering results in terrible consequences for understanding and usability when used for a non-trivial numbers of data objects.

This pursuit of correctness in this way makes things more difficult to understand in practice and lengthens time on task. Worse yet, making a visual chaos look "appealing" adversely affects things by distracting us from divining its meaning. We need to focus more on the significance of related elements without being overwhelmed by the visuals that connect them to each other, which is so often the case.

To alleviate this problem, our approach should be to illustrate relationships and connections by using progressive disclosure to surface details when needed, but lead with a clear overview and impression of the strength of connection and frequency of interaction vs. the entire depth of the graph.

Your eyes will thank us.

Examples

As always, the best way to see true impact is to compare how things were versus how they could be, or are now. In these examples, you'll see how leveraging aspects of visual systems provides an immediate boost to the speed of recognition and understanding.And it effectively piques interest.

Let's examine a few common areas of monitoring and reporting.

Dynamic Marketplaces are the canonical example of systems that could desperately use a standard visual representation which utilizes space and dimensionality. The problem is that until now, this has been done clumsily by extruding 2D charts and graphs into 3D objects. That approach doesn't add anything except visual noise. The new approach provides a tangible difference – we'll use an instantly recognizable metaphor to ground our depiction (so to speak), you'll see a floor plane with data objects on top, much like you'd see in a data scientist's living room (ok, maybe not quite yet ;-)

Modern Organizations have been represented by 1960's looking org charts for as long as anyone can remember. They work, but given the critical importance of understanding how people relate in our organizations, this is a huge oversight. There's never been an advance here (except by George Robertson of Microsoft Research in the early 2000's when he created a 3D organizational chart for the company as an internal experiment). By utilizing just a bit of spatialness, we not only get a better sense of the breadth of sprawling orgs, but also their relative depth, which quickly illuminates investments in headcount.

Real-Time Operations is probably the most fascinating area to see portrayed by visual systems. We have a natural attraction to seeing numbers, data, and state change as it happens. It's gratifying to have up-to-the-minute readouts on how things are going. Imagine seeing the progress of operations in a manufacturing plant in a highly visual way that corresponds to the physical layout, but it being overlayed with key metrics and data that embodies state. We'd be able to see the status like on a 2D dashboard today, but also visually align the data and information to where it's happening within the plant.

Summary

Visual Systems are the most immediate way to see and understand the current status of any business.

Innovative Approaches

Not "out of the box". Out of the blue.

Remember when we talked about being able to immediately spot true innovations because they're just so obvious? They seem very familiar, yet completely new and unbelievably cool. Somehow perfectly right. Nothing to consider or argue about – just take my money.

The following innovative approaches fall into that category of true breakthroughs that will undoubtably contribute to making 4D business systems ubiquitous and empowering. Each approach illustrates a foundational aspect of the "4D spreadsheet" or enables our ability to "play 4D chess", but they also show us how humankind continually pushes forward to achieve more than anyone ever thought possible.

Datascapes

There's an inescapable feeling that washes over you when first seeing data displayed in an immersive 3D space or projection. It just feels "right" when done well. Perhaps that's because of the extreme cool factor of looking at data escaping our flat screens. Or maybe we just couldn't imagine there being anything like this possible that made sense immediately.

Regardless of why, when data we recognize is finally brought to life in an immersive space, and it looks more like a beautiful sculpture than an Excel chart, we can't help but realize it should have always been like this.

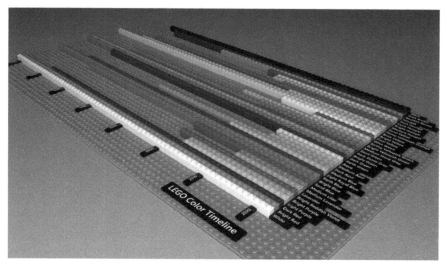

Histogram of Lego brick color introductions by decade
(Credit: Dave Brown, Microsoft Research)

A feeling of familiarity and connectedness is there right from the start. We recognize the shapes, volumes, and sizes of the data as we would a physical object in our office or home. The data objects seem to make sense immediately, even if we don't know anything about what they represent. We inherently understand spatial scenes by the way things relate to each other in adjacency, presence, and behavior. Immersive data spaces seem like a natural for us because they mimic the world we exist in.

Room-scale datascape being used for analysis and exploration

Consider how you'd feel when exposed to what I call "room scale data" – things that are literally as big as walls, entire floors, or even skyscrapers. It's both exhilarating and daunting. In an instant, the scale and magnitude of our data is made real for us and our understanding of the world. Using this deep immersion and freeform exploration to gain insight is where we're headed next when visualizing business.

"Datascapes" are immersive 3D spaces, both digital and physical, that represent the content and states of datasets.

Datascapes are designed to be viewed, explored, analyzed, and most importantly **experienced** to gain a much deeper understanding. That interaction leads to new insights, which come in ways only datascapes can deliver. Due to their unique properties, we are able to coexist with our data in the same way we do with any physical space.

Picking up data objects, comparing their sizes and relative weights, and interrogating them through normal conversation (thanks to Large Language Models and Generative AI chat interfaces) is why this so greatly differs from anything we've be accustomed to. Another example of how it should have always been, and now is.

Data Art

Large-scale data art installations are today's best examples of what can be accomplished with room-scale, AI-powered visual experiences. The rigor and scale of these technical marvels demonstrate the feel and impact of fully realized datascapes for 4D business visualization.

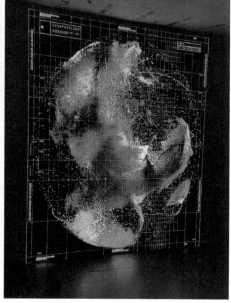

"Unsupervised" by Refik Anadol at MoMA in NYC

Refik Anadol is the undisputed world champion of bringing data to life. A renowned media artist and multi-disciplinary designer, his AI-powered large-scale data art installations have achieved legendary status. Found in every part of the globe, at varying scales, these data art pieces are unique in their appearance and aspirations – to make us dream. "Inspiring" doesn't even come close to describing the feeling you have when seeing his work unfold dynamically before you. The pieces are constantly in motion, continuously revealing new aspects, and gracefully morphing states, in the most fluid of ways imaginable.

Built upon gigantic datasets and manipulated in real-time by his team's custom AI algorithms, his data art creates a sense of wonder for his audience. The pieces quite often "break the plane", creating a feeling that the content has escaped the wall-sized framing and is coming outside its confines to perform for its audience.

Undulating, fluid-like shapes appear very photorealistic, while using physics, vivid colors, and visceral materiality to portray living data. Stunningly beautiful to behold and consider.

Refik's sublime data art pieces are not only inspiring a generation to learn more about data and art but offer a glimpse into the future of business communication. His many experiments have proven that an

AI-based approach to data visualization is viable and can be used to synthesize fluid forms that convey specific meaning. Refik's work is the first and best example of using AI to bring data to life, artistically for now, but clearly on a path that takes us to 4D business simulations. Thank you, Refik!

Light sculptures are another exciting glimpse into the future of business visualization and simulations. By using physical containers of light to display data and convey meaning, we are seeing how our innate understanding of the physical world and 3D objects can lead to deeper understanding. We naturally recognize what a great number of things in the physical world are trying to tell us, either intentionally or subliminally, just by their shape, color, and reaction to stimulus. That's the same principle we use when constructing "light sculptures" of data sets. Each shape displays what could be considered a chart or graph element, encoded with key information, in recognizable ways.

Data takes the form of a light sculpture for public consumption

Light sculptures provide a rich canvas for data exploration

Often used as corporate office sculptures, these art pieces are far more valuable to the organization and its guests than you'd first think. By embodying valuable corporate data within sculpture-like pieces, we take a physical approach to the presentation aspect of business communication. They also leave an impression that's hard to shake.

We'll eventually "read" these light sculptures just like you'd read wayfinding or flight status signage in airports today, particularly through the use of intuitive design. The key is to develop containers that are flexible enough to illustrate many diverse types of information and insights in a fixed physical environment. These seemingly decorative elements of public spaces will quickly become the new output device for your corporate data to be seen and appreciated by your customers and employees alike.

Soundscapes

Over the past decade, podcasts have emerged as a popular way to learn new things or catch up on current events while multitasking. These audio-only programs have earned a dedicated following and have even created their own subculture. In many ways, podcasts have brought back the immersive experience of early radio broadcasts, allowing listeners to create vivid "soundscapes" in their minds. Audio tends to cause our minds to create soundstages where the action unfolds over time – which sounds alot like what we've been describing throughout the book as the whole purpose of 4D visualizations.

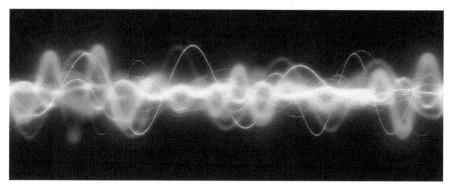

Soundscapes can visually depict emotion and feelings

This idea of sonic landscapes is not new. Many classical music compositions and classic rock "concept" albums transport listeners to another place and time through the power of sound. Adding real-time visuals to these soundscapes takes the experience to a whole new level of immersion, not unlike a live concert experience that's staged for maximum impact. In decades past, we've seen the emergence of audio visualizers in computer music apps and screensavers, as people liked "seeing" songs and sounds that are typically only heard. That trend is back in a startlingly new way.

The Apple TV+ series "Calls" debuted in 2021 and introduced a new paradigm for not only seeing auditory conversations, but viscerally feeling them. Through the brilliant use of animated vector graphics and spatial visual effects, the producers and designers of this futuristic series brought phone conversations between people to life in the most memorable way any of us have ever seen. It was astonishing how far they advanced the notion of "seeing" a phone call unfold in real-time. They gave the viewer the ability to not only follow along with the action but view the essence of the human emotion and relationship dynamics involved through their stunning visuals. It's quite startling to see human emotion visualized in this way.

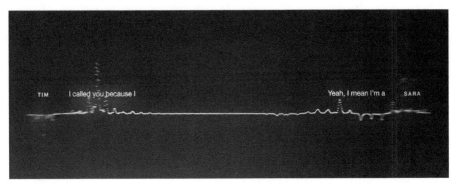

Seeing a conversation and emotion unfold from "Calls" on Apple TV+

Part of the beautiful execution of Apple TV+ *Calls* is its use of multi-modality to impart the information being conveyed. There are the primary audio tracks of the people's voices in the conversations, but also a real-time visual representation of the voice represented as a waveform, that is perfectly synced to the audio. And that's precisely where it goes way beyond what's expected. The waveform shows emotion and dynamics, expressed through shape, color, speed, and morphing, that bring the person and their state of mind to life in such a clear way, it's a bit unnerving. OK, I'll admit, it's very unnerving due to the great storylines.

The pioneering effort of *Calls* will clearly be the inspiration and possibly even the basis for how 4D conversations will be represented. It's that good. And that powerful. Do yourself a favor and watch an episode or two. I can't possibly describe how well done this is – you just have to see and hear it.

Embodiment

Often when dealing with something important in our lives, we'd much prefer talking to a person rather than struggling through a complicated online form or dealing with a bot. It's human nature. We like talking to people in these stressful situations. And so it is with our work and the future of business communication. We'll be collaborating with our teammates and partners all the time within 4D visualization systems, so the same desire to talk with people will exist when some of the interaction will be with AIs that are embodied as human-like.

There's no question that we're getting more comfortable dealing with machines and software much of the time, but there's something comforting about a human voice or face. This is why embodiment, or software taking the form of a human being, or humanoid-like entity, is important to the future of visualizing business. As we're running our what-if scenarios and presenting key insights, we'll sometimes need or want a "person" to interact with vs. a command line of bot text.

People want to talk with people. Our technology needs to embody a form that comes closer to real people for us to be satisfied.

Avatars have come a long way. What once were a joke because they appeared as crude cartoon-like figures, have recently evolved into highly photorealistic representations of real people, with eye blinking, convincing movements, and subtle mannerisms. In fact, you may be hard pressed to quickly spot whether a *MetaHuman* created in Unreal Engine isn't a real person. We've finally crossed the "uncanny valley", at least in the photorealistic avatar world. Robots may be next.

MetaHumans are photorealistic digital avatars
(Credit: Unreal Engine, Epic Games, Inc.)

Be on the lookout for your first encounter with a photorealistic avatar when you are trying to get help from your favorite store or service provider online. It won't be long now, and you may even like them and their voices.

Holograms are not new either, but still capture our imagination. Once seen as glitchy projected light fields (ala Princess Leia), they have progressed over the years from cartoonish lo-fi representations of people to what we have today – highly realistic projections using different techniques.

Holograms are similar in style and function to high quality avatars when used for presence. But recently, there's been a very innovative take on full-sized holograms for the business world that's literally turning heads. Video-based holograms are finally here.

The **ARHT Media Capsule** is a glass phonebooth-like device that beams high-quality video holograms into your office or conference. Whether using live video or pre-recorded takes, these are incredibly cool to interact with. It appears as if a real person is just inside the Capsule talking to you. And better yet, they can hear and see you as well to enable back and forth conversations. But it's much more than just a video hologram.

The Capsule by ARHT Media

Done using a setup similar to a motion capture studio, the person on the other end talks in front of a camera and computer that converts the video and audio into a lifelike hologram inside the Capsule on the other end. It's quite easy to use, and a real attraction once you've seen it. Again, our desire to talk with other human beings during business meetings and presentations will drive the use of these high-quality experiences. You'll be amazed by this, trust me.

Robots are not always the beginning of the end. I'm joking here. They're fine, really. In fact, some people will be more comfortable interacting with robots than other humans eventually. They'll be less creepy (I'm looking at you *Boston Dynamics* ;-) and a bit more empathetic as they learn to mimic human interactions. We should also expect relatable digital robots to appear within our spatial computing environments as assistants and coworkers.

Projection

Using clever 3D projection techniques to see content break out of its container is absolutely breathtaking. It's so easy to see how this is not going away anytime soon. We finally cracked the code on getting highly engaging 3D experiences in front of people without requiring special optics via glasses or headsets. The result is outstanding.

Holographic Billboards - Simultaneously shocking and thrilling when you first see them in action, 3D billboards are on fire. Mostly found in urban centers with huge outdoor screens like in downtown Tokyo, Times Square, or Piccadilly Circus, these billboards display super slick brand advertisements with a huge twist – the content "breaks the plane" and jumps right off the screen. It surprises you in a fun roller coaster kinda way. It's wild. And clearly the future of 3D immersion when personal optics are not possible.

3D breaking the plane of giant billboards for business

You'll often see the most ingenious cinematic sequences on these billboards that all use the same visual gag – they show what appears to be impossible, content comes right out of the screen into what you would swear was into the air or inside the building. Shapes and cutouts that clearly are not normal for flat sides of office buildings play host to all manner of creatures, products, and scenes that come to life, morph, and ultimately delight us in ways we didn't know existed.

This will be used for business visualization in numerous ways – first as branding and marketing of products and services, but just after we'll put insights and data through the same treatment to evoke that same emotional connection to land our points. These displays will be found on buildings, corporate headquarters, and campuses around the world in no time with the express purpose of helping convey business insights and cutting-edge advertisements.

What we normally just see as premium ad space will also be prime real estate for experimenting with business data and messaging. With so much corporate messaging focused on sustainability and social good issue, these high impact surfaces are perfect for delivering a new kind of comms experience aimed at memorability and impact.

Floor-based Projections – We have experimented for some time with immersive experiences that project imagery onto the floor. These are mostly entertainment and art-related installations that use ceiling mounted projectors to drive the illumination. Fascinating to watch, people are drawn to the floor plane being the center of attention for these rudimentary projection systems.

What we are looking at now is utilizing that same fascination with the floor plane combined with room-scale data to create immersive data walk-throughs. In the same way that datascapes provide a new level of understanding, walking amongst your data is a revelation.

Using the floor plane for projection allows for no glasses immersion
(Credit: Dave Brown, Microsoft Research, M. Pell)

Just as it's normal and expected to walk around an art installation or interactive museum piece, being able to experience information in this way brings the added benefit of us naturally recognizing the scale and relationships between objects. The fact that its living data is the innovation here. We'll be able to use these floor plane projected spaces to play out scenarios, much like an oversized chess set in a park.

3D Tablets and Phones - No longer just a novelty, small tablets and monitors that can display stereoscopic 3D with no special glasses have taken a huge leap forward as well. You can now see the same kind of plane-breaking 3D effects as with the much larger 3D billboards on what look like ordinary Android tablets and computer monitors. By using a technique that requires some special hardware integrated into the screen, we can enjoy gaming, movies, and visualizations that pop out of the screen, and don't' require any special glasses or headsets at all. This is a jaw-dropping experience when you first see it, but more importantly, it's exactly how immersive business visualizations will come to the mainstream.

The Leia, Inc. "no glasses" 3D tablet

Leia, Inc. has created an outstanding no-glasses 3D tablet that redefines spatial content creation and consumption. Their *Lume Pad* is incredibly fun to use and show off you really won't want to put it down.

Just as we've been talking about throughout this book, Leai, Inc. has used advanced AI and nanotech to synthesize 3D content from standard photos, videos, and generative art. Their innovative hardware approach is called Diffractive Lightfield Backlighting™ (DLB), which utilizes a special layer that meshes with the display screen. Coupled with AI-powered software to generate the spatialized content on the fly, their system feels right, even in its early stages.

It's spectacular to behold taking any existing YouTube video and converting it almost immediately to spatial 3D on their tablet. The tablet works like any other with touchscreen, pinch and zoom, accelerometer for sensing motion, and the ability to use it in 2D only mode anytime. Mind blowing coolness.

Even better is when you use the onboard cameras to create natively 3D spatial photos and videos to share with others who have the same device. This really does evoke an emotional reaction, it's that compelling – which is why we're betting on this tech for business visualization and data storytelling.

The company formerly known as **Dimenco** has merged with Leia, Inc. to bring their Simulated Reality technology to larger computer displays to create a no-glasses required viewing experience that feels just like you're in an IMAX 3D theater, but again, no glasses required. You can immediately feel as you sit in front of one of these 3D displays that we are moving into a new phase of immersion. I've watched so many people have the same reaction – first, disbelief of what they're seeing, then amusement as they run through all the possibilities in their minds.

Leia/Dimenco display's Simulated Reality™

Watching Blu-ray 3D films, playing a VR-enabled game, or being able to move objects in the air just by moving your hands (sensors built in) is beyond cool – it's game-changing for the engineering and entertainment industry.

Having access to a large computer display like this one immediately makes you think of how cool it would be to replace your 4K TV with one as well – but for the moment, this is a single person experience, as the depth sensing cameras on the front bezel are tracking your eyes in order to find the perfect viewing angle to create the spatial 3D effect. Perhaps multi-person will be in a future version, but for now, it's incredibly impressive as a solo experience.

Summary

Many new-to-world innovations comprise the foundational elements of 4D simulations and business visualization

Responsible Designs

We control how all this unfolds

Despite what you may have read, we do in fact have the power and skill to create AI-based 4D systems that behave themselves – meaning they act in an ethical manner and don't end up causing more harm than good. The key of course, is to keep humans in charge. We cannot allow ourselves to become so complacent with early success that we let the machines to do everything autonomously for us just because it's easier that way. We've all seen how that movie ends. I'm all for streamlining and automation wherever it makes sense – but this is different.

Just about any AI expert will tell you the same thing – people need to be in the loop at key points. Yes, these AI systems are approaching magical capabilities in many ways, but we have got to pay closer attention to what is generated by our new AI-powered tools, correct them, and even stop the proceedings when it appears things are not as expected. That's an inescapable responsibility, at least for now.

Giving humans an oversight and approval role in any AI system makes a ton of sense. It's exactly the kind of thing we're good at – review and approval vs. continual monitoring. They do that really well. And machines certainly don't get as distracted and tired as we tend to. So, it seems like a perfect division of responsibilities. Not to mention people have a natural ability to apply some degree of morality and ethics throughout the process.

And it's that last part, morality and ethics, where these 4D systems will earn their stripes as being responsible. They may exceed any initial expectations we have for them in terms of performance and output, but without the semblance of a soul they may continue to feel too mechanical. That's not an issue for some people as output is the key for them, but we've got to look past the efficiency to the heart of the matter. People are always more important than technology. These systems must reflect their usage as trusted collaborators.

To assist us getting to the future with our ethics intact, there are some design principles we need to keep in mind as we build out and use these 4D visualization systems.

The pillars of Responsible Design for 4D systems

Design Principles

Over the last several years, **Microsoft** has developed and refined a set of *Responsible AI principles* the company uses to guide the thinking and development of its new services and data analytics. Paraphrased below and adapted to the development and use of 4D business visualization and simulation systems, these should be kept in mind as we develop these transformational business systems.

Fairness – ensure these systems treat all individuals fairly and without bias, by avoiding unfair discrimination and mitigating the impact of potential biases in data and algorithms used throughout. As we explore distinct aspects of our businesses, we must be careful not to depict people and situations without some reflection on whether we'd consider it a fair assessment given all the factors.

Reliability & Safety – prioritize the development of 4D systems that operate reliably and safely, meaning they strive to minimize errors, mitigate risks, and ensure robustness in deployment and delivery of key business information. Just as we've added rigor to the performance and reliability of cloud-based systems, we also need to build in the safety aspects that include people in the process for double checks and approval.

Privacy & Security – we must commit to protecting the privacy and security of an individual's data when using these new AI-powered technologies. They must implement strong security measures and adhere to privacy regulations. There will be continual concern about any enterprise data escaping outside the corporate firewall, and in the same way, we also need to ensure that an individual's accounts are afforded the same level of protection.

Inclusiveness – be dedicated to creating 4D business systems that are accessible and inclusive. Ensure the combined technologies don't discriminate or exclude individuals based on factors such as race, gender, or disability. The data that's been used to train the model is often cited as the problem here, and it is, but there's also the ability for us to program in an approach that strives to be inclusive regardless of the corpus used.

Transparency – strive to provide transparency regarding the design, implementation, and performance of the AI and models used in the systems. Explain the decision-making process of AI models and make it understandable to anyone. This also applies to where the data comes from that's being used for the historical walkthroughs and simulations. Just like in journalism where sources are cited, these systems need to have data source references available, and offer visual representation of where data was sourced or resides.

Accountability – take responsibility for the impact and outcomes of these new combined technologies. Work to establish mechanisms for accountability that also address any unintended consequences or harm caused by the AI or data in these systems. Frequently talked about, but seldom followed through on, being accountable in business is rare. It happens when people decide to do the right thing, which can happen more often if designed into the process. We have an obligation to guide the design of these world-changing systems to be responsible and hold those who use and control them accountable.

Other Considerations

We should also discuss a few other areas that are pertinent to our responsible design efforts.

Clarity – Part of being responsible is being clear. And it's that core principle of striving to be clear that will ultimately allow these systems to become trusted partners. There's a big difference between being detailed and being clear. Throwing a bunch of interesting information into the workspace without organizing it into a clear message and perspective helps no one.

How will we clarify the inherent chaos in our systems?
(Credit: Dave Brown, Microsoft Research)

Similarly, leveraging the ability for these systems to present data in beautiful ways that can distract from the key message is a constant temptation. As always, it's more important to be clear than beautiful. So, the design of these systems need to combine those two thoughts into one – be beautifully clear.

Persuasion – One of the massive advances in communication found in these 4D visualization systems is their ability to effortlessly persuade through a ground-breaking approach to visual presentation of data. That's also the biggest threat posed by these new tools. It's relatively straightforward to manipulate how information will be perceived by tailoring the methods and techniques used by these advanced systems. Whether that's appearance, focus, movement, or narrative, anything can be altered to intentionally shift thinking.

There's nothing wrong with persuading responsibly, as popular advertisements have shown over time, but this practice is different. Our temptation to use this powerful new capacity to persuade without any regard to the implied ethics or outcome, is a challenge for us all to deeply consider. Just because we can, doesn't mean we should.

Trust – As we discussed earlier, ultimately this is all about us being able to rely on these new business visualization systems in the same way you would a trusted colleague. They will be used all the time to create the reports we'll take action on, and base decisions on.

Given their anticipated role within global business, we need to design in responsible practices and processes that result in predictable and reliable output. It's critically important to deliver on this – because the alternative is bad decisions based on misleading information. Focusing on delivering systems that deserve our trust will make all the difference. And when we achieve that level of trustworthiness, these digital tools will become true collaborators, just like our teammates.

Sentiment – It's hard to not see the anxiety and fear many people have when seeing what technology is capable of these days. It's real and it's not going away. Seems that tech has finally crossed over into being a true threat to humanity – at least from the perspective of many. Given that we need to keep a close eye on the sentiment of the public at large. People are at the center of everything we do, and this is all freaking them out. Even some highly knowledgeable practitioners are starting to sound the alarm. We have to stay in touch to be responsible.

There are many real issues to contend with when trying to deploy world-changing technologies, and many of them land squarely in this space – accountability, taking people's jobs, discrimination, consent, surveillance, mistakes, bias, aggression, and greed to name just a few.

As we continue to explore and build out these new systems for the good of all, staying close to the sentiment of our friends, families, neighbors, and people we will probably never meet in other parts of the world, is absolutely critical to our success. We need to be great listeners and act upon the sentiment found surrounding what we may be enamored with, rather than brushing it off as non-believers or just not knowledgeable about all this.

People are worried. And we should be, too.

Summary

Faced with the ability to persuade at will, it is our responsibility to ensure these 4D systems behave ethically

PART 3

POWERED BY

VISUALIZING BUSINESS

Breakthrough Technologies

Behind the curtain of the great and powerful Oz

It's become a full-time job trying to keep up with all the AI-related advancements happening each day. People say we're currently living through what's called a "stacked exponential" innovation curve, or an almost unbelievable rate of change. In practical terms, that means AI advances are coming at such a rapid pace it's almost impossible to pinpoint where we're at exactly from an overview level. It's a bit scary to acknowledge this is all too fast to track, but it's also quite thrilling to experience. The possibilities seem limitless.

One of the most exciting parts of what's been happening recently in tech is that we've finally been able to develop and combine the key foundational pieces of visualizing business using this new approach:

Artificial Intelligence   **Data Visualization**
Spatial Computing   **Bandwidth**
Web3   **Audio**
Simulation   **Devices**

Let's look at a few examples of these individual pieces, then the combination in action.

Artificial Intelligence

Where do we start? Since I typed in these words you're reading, the AI world has catapulted forward so many times it's hard to identify breakthroughs that will be truly enduring versus incremental innovation. Some will morph almost immediately into an even more powerful or flexible form. Others will set a direction to be run down by scores of efforts that follow.

These are a few of the AI-powered innovations that will continue to be very useful when building out the capabilities required for 4D business simulations. The key aspect of these is their ability to assist with data analysis, perform actions, and create projections.

Microsoft Copilot is an AI-powered assistance service that acts as a trusted collaborator and assistant to your common tasks. It has been deeply integrated across most of the common Microsoft applications and web services we use every day. Web search, meetings, creating content, working with financial data, coding, security, and even web browsing have all been augmented with something that feels very much like a brilliant coworker who can have contextually relevant conversations about our current work, and help get tasks done with incredible speed and quality.

We cannot overstate the significance of this recent addition to the Microsoft suite of applications and Azure Cloud services. It's game-changing to the point of almost being unbelievable. We have shifted from needing to do almost everything manually to having the choice to have the system do things with us or for us, super well, very fast.

Microsoft Copilots are critically important to the type of work we do with 4D Visualizations and Simulations. They provide the ability to deeply explore, question, and quickly modify these representations of our businesses. Copilot tech can transform these 4D workspaces into the ultimate What-If machines. Anything is possible when you have an assistant that tries its best to accommodate any request.

Autonomous Agents like *AutoGPT* enable us to direct an AI to automatically complete tasks to achieve a specified goal. These "autonomous agents" are not unlike Agent Smith from *The Matrix*, meaning they are potentially scary entities. You could choose to have an AI work independently on completing a goal by chaining a set of smaller tasks together. If it got stuck, it would figure out how to proceed by trying new paths, and keep on going until it completed the directive (unless it was completely blocked in some way).

The huge innovation here is not having to tell the AI what to do at every step via prompt engineering. You can specify a goal and have the system work on accomplishing it by itself. These sessions won't always be able to continue on without some input or intervention from people, but they are getting more clever about finding ways to press forward with the addressing the assigned goal.

In dystopian sci-fi movies, this is the exact scenario where an AI that's not being monitored closely starts doing things that are harmful and unexpected. But presently, it's still early days and people are not prone to enable the AI systems to do non-trivial tasks on their own without human monitoring or approval gates.

ModuleQ is a contextually-aware AI-based business service that proactively surfaces key insights to prepare employees for upcoming customer and client interactions. Built on the basic principles of Smart Information covered in my last book, this technology goes deep in its analysis of what would best setup success for people who need to keep on top of breaking news, trends, financial data, and previous insights – then delivers them in preferred channels for consumption. The difference with ModuleQ and other Generative AI systems is the focus on highly relevant data tailored exclusively to your work and history versus general information.

The way ModuleQ actively surfaces insights before they are asked for is at the very heart of what makes 4D systems so different than existing business analytics tools – they anticipate and act. In this case, gathering items dynamically to help prepare us for situations we don't even realize are about to happen.

Data Visualization

Fundamentally unchanged for decades, we are all still using the same basic charts and graphs as we always have. Fortunately, the field of data science and visualization has been seeing some very welcome advances lately. The most significant of which is the ability to make the presentation and exploration of the data itself more interesting – even to those who aren't familiar with the subject matter. This is why 4D systems represent such a giant leap forward - they capture our imagination and attention, encouraging us to explore and experiment with "what-if" scenarios to see how the images transform into even more intriguing forms.

WebGPU is one of the biggest advancements in the rendering of 3D graphics ever. Developed to draw super high-quality 3D scenes within a web page, this cloud-based technology eliminates the need to have a GPU (Graphics Processing Unit) chip in the local device but will take advantage of one if it exists. This is truly game changing for the types of applications we're working with, where 3D visual quality is paramount. What it means in practical terms is that a device with no GPU onboard will still display stunning visual renderings in real-time.

Imagine being able to play the most photorealistic looking 3D game you have ever seen on a normal tablet or smartphone. That's just not possible today, but it will be. And it will be just as satisfying as if you had played it on a high-end game console. If you know anything about 3D hardware that sounds ridiculous, I know. But, it's real and available now to all of us. And better yet, with the addition of 5G mobile bandwidth, the gameplay and interaction is just as fast as you'd expect on a wired ethernet connection.

Next gen business visualization is dependent on this type of high-speed, high-quality approach to rendering 3D graphics. WebGPU is a key tech advancement we should be utilizing wherever possible to ensure a consistent feel when working with these data visualizations and business simulations.

MorphCharts is a research project from the brilliant Dave Brown of Microsoft Research which showcases leading edge visualization work done with a web-based 3D rendering library that uses raytracing to create ultra high-quality visualization. These fresh takes on data representation use materials, motion blur, depth of field, and exquisite typography to create magnificent imagery. *RTViz* is the code library being used as a showcase for exploring the aesthetic properties of data visualization. Available via open source.

I find this work so incredibly inspiring that many of the visually striking data illustrations in this book have been done with Dave's RTViz library. His work is truly groundbreaking in the field and will be recognized as having significant impact as we all leap forward into the world of 4D business visualization.

Spatial Computing

Everything you use on a flat screen today is heading toward being experienced in 3D. It's a self-fulfilling prophecy that our next huge shift in computing after cloud will be spatial (i.e. 3D). We've all been working toward this for decades. Why? Because we live in a 3D world, we innately understand it, and are still incredibly fascinated with replicating it digitally. Go figure.

You may have heard the term "Metaverse" used alot the last few years and more recently the phrase "Spatial Computing" from Apple. In the simplest terms, both refer to using a 3D interface to interact with and experience what's normally 2D screen-based activities. Imagine taking today's phone, web, and game experiences and morphing them all into 3D versions of themselves.

Spatial computing is a general category descriptor like "mobile computing" or "cloud computing". The spatial part refers to a new interaction paradigm where everything you deal with from apps to the operating system itself is in 3D. The computing part refers to the medium and platform itself. Think of this in the same way as mobile computing relies on smartphones, and cloud computing relies on datacenters. Spatial computing relies on 3D.

The Metaverse on the other hand can best be described as a 3D version of the Web. It encompasses all the good things the Web has evolved into over time, with its most important aspect being its open nature. Games and social networks are good examples of what the Metaverse promises to reimagine in a more immersive, 3D way.

Fortunately for us, the core technologies used in both the Spatial Computing and Metaverse visions are the same, and make up the key components of 4D systems - immersion, animation, sound, motion, collaboration, social interaction, and performance.

3D Platforms

Here are a few breakthrough platforms and tech that will help to power the future of business visualization with 4D:

Apple visionOS - touted as the first spatial operating system for the spatial computing headset called *Apple Vision Pro*, visionOS has a real chance becoming the first OS to achieve widespread adoption as a consumer experience over the next several years. This is due in part to the failure of other VR headsets to break out of niche use (by gamers and hobbyists) into general computing. The other factor is quality. Apple did its homework as usual and as is its style, combined many of the best advanced technologies into one sleek device and delivered a pro level software development kit (SDK) and developer program. Time will tell how this developer platform evolves, but it will certainly catalyze a new generation of stellar work.

4D business visualization and simulation systems will be best experienced on streamlined devices like the Apple Vision Pro running visionOS. It's just too bad we're still dealing with a relatively bulky headset vs lightweight glasses or projection system, for now.

Unreal and **Unity** are modern game engines that have elevated the art of game development to unimaginable heights in the last few years. What was widely considered almost impossible twenty years ago is now their specialty – rendering photorealistic 3D graphics in real-time, that utilize realistic lighting, shadows, and convincing physics engines. This can all be done for multiple players, across every major device, from smartphones to consoles to laptops. And all with the ability to create multi-player experiences for any purpose.

And while most people consider these game engines, they should be thought of as the ultimate platforms for visualization. Both are the ultimate foundation for the kinds of business simulations we have been discussing. There couldn't be a richer palette for immersion, aesthetics, and interaction.

What Unity and Unreal deliver as content is closer to a cinematic movie experience than a traditional computer game in many instances. They both are fully featured development environments, supporting next generation functionality for gaming, collaboration, and simulation. And they are both the right choice for doing Spatial Computing development.

LAMINA1 is building an open Metaverse platform for creators to participate in the next wave of immersive experiences. More than just another startup, one founder literally coined the term Metaverse many years ago, another created it from both a conceptual and technological perspective, and the other was an early cryptocurrency pioneer. Their company's vision and mission is heady – a decentralized, fair, and high performing platform for people to build the future of everything. The architecture of this new platform is intended to serve as the basis for the next generation of experiences that need real-time performance from blockchain and immersive 3D environments.

Because of its focus on state-of-the-art platform architecture for distributed, decentralized, crypto-enabled, performant experiences, LAMINA1 will be the choice for business visualization services that want to draw on the best of the creator economy in a transparent, equitable way. It's the best of us, all in one platform.

Web3

There's been much talk and confusion about the third iteration of the World Wide Web (aka. Web3). Suffices to say it's a loose collection of useful approaches to online community building powered by modern technologies supporting a more decentralized Web. Monetization and equitable stewardship are among the key concepts underlying this version. Web3 serves our vision of 4D experiences by contributing some of the best new technologies and architecture into our toolsets for visualizing business.

Microtransactions are the part of cryptocurrencies that matter the most to what we'll be doing with 4D simulations. A microtransaction is remarkably simple to describe – the ability to charge less than a US dollar or any major unit of fiat currency. That means you can charge me less than a penny for something – but to date, it's been too difficult to implement at scale. It's a very old concept (more than 30 years), but hard to deliver on due to the computational and transactional costs not being low enough to make it feasible, even on a worldwide volume basis. That will change soon, but for now it remains a lofty goal.

The reason we need microtransactions as part of our 4D business system architectures is to enable the acquisition of data at fractional costs to round out scenarios, simulations, and what-if queries. The systems we build will need to pull data on-demand, which means being able to compensate the data's owners extremely fast, at very low overhead costs for the transactions. Companies may be more incented to share valuable data if they can increase their profits by breaking down the datasets into individual datapoints or small groups vs. large collections. By getting more granular, they can securely sell much more on-demand via microtransaction systems.

Blockchain is a database-like technology closely associated with Web3 and cryptocurrency. A distributed digital ledger that is intended to be completely transparent for both record keeping and verification of ownership, blockchains are the basis for many online marketplaces and transactional communities such as NFTs. The value to business visualization systems is the ability to keep scenarios and data on the blockchain to promote the notion of open and transparent, cooperative simulation systems that are accessible by entities both inside and outside of your own organization.

Part of the value here is knowing that a dataset or piece of content has been published and verified on a public blockchain using **identity** services and can be trusted as the basis for historical rewinds or predicted futures. The verification and transparency of all information associated with a visualization or simulation helps to create a "trusted source" situation for news and data, much like we had with major news outlets before the rise of highly skewed opinions and fake news. Companies will require using trusted sources when ingesting data for use in their own simulations and visualizations.

Simulation

Much of this book is focused on how to simulate business process at a global scale, which is an incredibly big challenge for myriad reasons – computational cost, data access, storage, verification, visualization requirements, etc. Yet, simulation is the very cornerstone of 4D, and something that needs to be as performant and secure as possible. To that end, a few outstanding cloud-based platforms help us achieve what we know is possible – a 1:1 simulation of our business scenarios using digital twins of the real world where available, and generating synthetic data where none exists.

Omniverse by NVIDIA is an industrial-strength 3D computing platform capable of doing massive scale simulations. These 3D scenes are modeled, rendered, and lit in a photorealistic way – but more importantly for us they can consume and work with Enterprise data sources. Designed to run in real-time, Omniverse can simulate things as varied as product configurators, gaming, and even represent entire manufacturing plants in operation with detailed activity happening within assembly lines. The level of detail here is astounding.

The Omniverse platform was designed with Spatial Computing and the Metaverse in mind, ready to be applied to very large-scale simulations using digital twins of physical spaces. Within these highly detailed 3D universes there exists the means to carefully instrument and closely measure the performance of objects and systems. That capacity alone makes Omniverse a perfect candidate platform to use for advanced business visualizations. Yet, it's only one of the many reasons Omniverse is the center of the simulation universe.

Omniverse environments and simulations can be quite real, not just approximations. That's so incredibly important for the success of 4D business simulations – being able to trust the simulation to use real data and behave in a predictable manner. Until the randomness of business kicks in, as always. Still, simulation is the future of business.

Bandwidth

We've all heard of 5G (Fifth Generation) wireless services by now as it relates to our smartphones. It's theoretically a much faster cellular network and promises to eventually revolutionize the types of things we can do with mobiles. The way 5G directly figures into visualizing business applications is its ability to greatly accelerate the streaming of data from the Cloud to the devices we all use. It also enables a shift to do some of the computing locally by pushing tasks down from the Cloud to a device to be closer to where the action is happening. Both of those capabilities reduce network latency and lowers costs through effective sharing of network resources.

Edge computing assisted by AI is considered by many to be the key to unlocking innovation across industries. This includes real-time tracking and control of autonomous vehicles and running high-quality simulations locally on mobile devices. These types of capabilities are greatly enhanced by using high-speed, ultra-low latency 5G networks.

One technique, multi-access edge computing (MEC) decentralizes the computing of traffic and services from the Cloud to the network's edge on people's devices. One of Asia's largest providers, Singtel, is collaborating with Microsoft and NVIDIA to combine AI and 5G, enabling enterprises to accelerate our mobile experiences by using Edge computing for bandwidth intensive applications like optimized real-time video streaming from live events and more life-like avatars with no visible lag.

Audio

The constantly overlooked element of any great experience is sound. It's one of the strongest indicators of state we have, as it instantly conveys a visceral feeling message. We are all hardwired to react immediately to audio cues. We'll leverage that natural alerting and status recognition system when presenting and exploring our business scenarios.

Dolby ATMOS and **Apple Spatial Audio** are notable examples of how far digital technologies have taken sound experiences for movies, music, and even podcasts. By using cinematic techniques to separate individual tracks, voices, and effects, the listener can interpret sound as we normally do in the physical world. It also creates a state where we can better understand and more deeply feel what's happening.

That's exactly the kind of emotive tech we want to employ in our 4D business simulations. We want to feel the status changes without even having to look at the screen. Sound can do that easily for us, but only if done well. It turns out that audio is perhaps the most powerful of mediums, but it's also the easiest to get wrong. Just as movie studios used highly skilled folly artists to recreate sound effects, and music engineers have become expert at editing sound, our 4D business simulations require that level of sonic wizardry.

Devices

The foundational element you cannot get away from in these advanced systems is unsurprisingly 3D. Dimensionality and immersion is the basis for Spatial computing, which brings us a whole new perspective on information and data. Until now, we've either had to settle for seeing 3D trapped within flat screens on our TVs, tablets, or phones for games, or experience it while forced to wear bulky VR headsets.

What's always been missing is a sleek form factor like glasses to make immersive apps a more enjoyable experience while looking super cool (instead of super dorky). This quest to miniaturize and lighten the electronics has been the focus of the tech industry over the last decade. We are finally getting somewhere, but not fast enough for anyone. Bulky headsets and goggles are still de rigueur for Spatial Computing, Mixed Reality, or Virtual Reality. But recently, a set of innovative approaches have inverted the model to bring immersive 3D graphics to people without the need for us to wear special glasses or massive headsets.

In addition to lightweight eyewear, there have been a number of research developments in the area of developing contact lenses for Augmented Reality. By projecting light fields onto the lens itself, we can emulate what happens with some types of glasses and headsets. This approach is extremely challenging from both a technical and physiological perspective, but seems to be the consensus for where these specialty optics devices will eventually end up converging.

Glimpses of 4D

After reading the previous descriptions of the breakthrough tech that will power the future of business visualization, it's time to pull it all together with an example of what's possible when we combine and focus them on a new experience for global business – exploring data using Artificial Intelligence.

Flow Immersive is a stunning example of how to create a data exploration system that has deeply integrated Generative AI into its standard experience. By using AI to provide active assistance during visualization explorations, Flow helps to uncover data insights and communicate key information in a very satisfying way through a wide variety of devices. Flow Immersive makes it easy to freely explore different properties and dimensions of just about any dataset in beautifully rendered forms such as maps, spatial timelines, and other innovative 3D data representations.

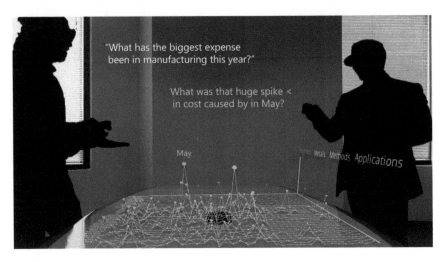

Using AI within Flow Immersive to actively assist with data exploration
(Credit: Flow Immersive, M. Pell)

Flow has always been in the vanguard of data exploration tools. A favorite of mine for its ability to simplify importing and working with data, it deserves to be recognized for quickly adopting this more conversational approach to data visualization. It has also used a superior text rendering technique for high quality typography for years, making the rendered information so much easier to read when in the headset.

Flow is the closest service we have available today to the futuristic 4D business visualization systems described in this book.

Summary

The optimal implementation of 4D business systems will combine technology elements of AI, Spatial Computing, Web3, Simulation, Data Visualization, Bandwidth, and Audio.

Cinematic Techniques

There's a reason we all love the movies

Film is one of those uniquely human things. It brings out our emotions, good or bad, and pulls us right into stories in a way few other things can. Directors use their craftsmanship to weave compelling stories that keeps our attention over hours. But, just like many other big industries, moviemaking is having its AI moment. Innovative tools that deliver ultra-high end cinematic effects are out there and are threatening to democratize filmmaking, just as it happened with the music industry via laptop studios. Guess what field is next?

Cinematic techniques for storytelling, aesthetics, and impact have finally come to the business world. And they are critical to building effective 4D visualization systems. We're not talking about creating high-end vision videos and glossy executive puff pieces though. We'll use a cinematic approach to infuse emotion into the chart and graph world. Information design and data presentation will never be quite the same.

It used to be delivering data via reports, charts, and graphs was strictly an exercise in objectivity and restraint. Completely plain, with no flair or hint of persuasion that would unduly influence people or trying to manipulate the facts. Data Scientists and Researchers were so hesitant to inject any of their own thinking or insights into reports, that it just wasn't done – that would be sacrilege. It would no longer be considered objective. We can't have opinions about data.

Well, that was then, and this is now. Like so many other areas AI has touched, the game has changed, and that taboo of only being objective is gone. Business as usual has evolved to embrace a more cinematic flair that's coming to your next team presentation.

Much more than asking ChatGPT to make your slides for you or getting DALL-E to update the images, the use of cinematic techniques to capture the viewer's attention and keep them riveted has opened the door to more movie-like experiences, even within previously cut and dry reporting. Where we used to rely on boring spreadsheet reports and tired old dashboards, there's something the industry calls "data storytelling" to use as a narrative assistant for presenting data in a more meaningful way. Think of charts as "scenes" not just static diagrams.

As we create this new visual data culture, all of the cinematic-style techniques and effects listed here will have a very particular role to play in conveying meaning and helping lead our audience to a deeper understanding:

Movement	**Typography**
Materiality	**Composition**
Lighting	**Soundscapes**
Motion Blur	**Multi-Dimensionality**
Depth of Field	

Cinematic effects transform graphs into motion picture quality frames
(Credit: Dave Brown, Microsoft Research, M. Pell)

Most often these effects work in tandem to amplify each other's strengths. Combining channels can help create an incredibly impactful moment when making a point, but they've got to be well-integrated to come across properly.

Just as we rarely notice a movie's dramatic soundtrack or lighting effects because they are blended so well into the scenes, our cinematic effects also need to be perfectly balanced and integral, not calling too much attention to themselves.

Movement

Few things convey meaning more clearly than motion. It's how we all come to understand the world. So, it's only natural that we'd rely on movement to represent flow, state, and intent within spatial systems. Whether seen or not, so many aspects of the most common activities are all about the **movement** of people, resources, materials, or money. We just tend to not think of it that way.

Showing how parts move along within a supply chain is an easy-to-understand example of *linear movement*. You can imagine a simple diagram that shows the flow of items throughout their journey to final assembly and sale. This simple movement could take the form of an animated process flowchart or something more location-based such as a map. It's also easy to picture being able to freeze that movement-based animation to locate individual objects at any point in time, or rewind the journey to verify status at various checkpoints.

Using movement in visualization advances our understanding of state by assigning motion to objects that are not generally considered "living" or even reactive in most cases. We recognize an object's function through simple motion, like flicking a light switch up and down signals on/off. Intent becomes clear through movement as well. For instance, sensing a predator's intent to eat you when it starts to lurch forward is pretty immediate. Adding these motion-based cues to data objects helps depict their role within a business ecosystem.

Another example of movement leading to insight is to use it as an indicator for effectiveness. For example, when looking at the communication within our teams, we can animate the movement of messaging, mails, and sharing of documents between teammates. By analyzing the flow and pace of them, we can shed light on the overall connectedness of the team, or lack thereof. Used this way, the motion itself isn't the focus, but rather what it represents (regular or spurious) that actually brings valuable insight.

Our businesses are constantly in motion. Now our data will be as well
(Credit: Dave Brown, Microsoft Research)

Materiality

Another missing element in standard reporting is any semblance of a visual aesthetic that enhances the impact or clarity of the message. In general, our industry has done an inadequate job of providing visually impactful elements (other than canned templates) over the years. Even the typography used in reports, charts, and diagrams isn't that great. We're not talking about just providing better layout and graphic design though – it has more to do with creating visual interest while adding an entirely new dynamic – visually encoded meaning.

What's been hiding in plain sight forever is our natural tendency to derive meaning from the **material** that something is made out of. Texture is such an integral part of our lives in so many ways – it's why we desire certain things and reject others. We are naturally wired to recognize textures immediately. Shiny? The thing is probably metallic or glassy. Rough? Probably durable and often used. Soft? Probably warm to the touch. There are so many examples of how we make quick assumptions about the quality of something based on its materials and texture. In this case, first impressions are truly the ones that matter.

Materiality is everything in luxury product design. So, it should be no surprise that we are leveraging that innate understanding of the qualities of fabric and materials to suggest characteristics of our data and information. Those encodings can range from thinking a shiny, deeply reflective material is high quality, to seeing a torn and creased cardboard surface as implying it's cheap. Something that looks like it's made from gleaming diamonds or gold will be regarded differently than the same object or dataset rendered in plastic. For better or worse, we almost automatically assign value based on visual appearance.

Applying this cognitive insight about materials to visualization is straightforward, but requires some experimentation to get right. There are obvious wins here when you can match the desired effect to the inherent qualities of the material. Each material has something it is best at conveying, so the craft is aligning the desired outcome to the immediate impression of the materials used. Care should be taken to not overuse this power to the point of being annoying or blatantly disregarding taste, i.e. being too flashy in certain situations that call for a more toned-down look.

You can almost feel the plastic of these data objects

Lighting

Another hugely important aspect of cinema is how scenes are lit. Used to focus attention, distract, or enhance the setting for action, lighting a scene properly is fundamental to success. And so it is with business visualizations. Great **lighting** draws our eye to the elements we need to see first. This is the same for any well-designed composition within the creative fields. Unfortunately for business-related uses, this type of attention to lighting is only found within custom 3D animations or high-end product renderings. That needs to change.

Need to punch up a particular insight or data point? Shine a spotlight or two onto it. Trying to emphasize how nothing in particular should stand out in a report? Make everything evenly lit with a soft ambient glow. Want to leave people with an emotional impression? Use colored lighting to evoke a particular emotion or mood within the scene, as is done expertly in the *John Wick* film series.

And finally, remember that just about any amount of lighting will immediately bring more attention and visual interest to your message. We are so adept at understanding the role of lighting, its effects are often immediate. Lighting can add drama, joy, or depth to any scene.

Motion Blur

Capturing movement in a still photo often shows **motion blur,** or the ghosted trail of an object that's moving from one position to another. It's literally the visual evidence of movement. When designing a system that relies on movement to communicate meaning, it's quite important to have a plan for how to still convey that when the scene is paused or shared as a static image. This is where motion blur helps signal things are moving and changing within a static chart or diagram.

It's uncanny how we immediately recognize what the motion blur is representing. For an object or collection of things, our brains fill in the details when seeing it rendered with motion blur. It should become a heavily used special effect in visual systems where elements are continuously moving, as it provides a visual cue as to how fast things are flowing. Seeing an elongated blur as a trail reads as an object or collection speeding along over time, while a short trail or faded image tends to signal very slow or previous movement.

One of the unexpected outcomes of rendering motion blur within running animations is it tends to be worth the expense, as it enhances the perception of movement for the viewer, even though it's computationally expensive.

Depth of Field

A tried-and-true photographic technique used to focus your attention on the foreground or background of a scene is called **depth of field**. It blurs the area of a scene that's not the center of interest. The amount of blur and its relative darkness helps enhance the impact.

We'll use depth of field in a similar fashion to direct the audience's initial focus of attention to the area of the data scene that conveys the most important detail. The other areas can still be seen through a blur or fog, helping to create context, but our attention is effectively drawn immediately. You'll sometimes see the focus shift from foreground to background in films to assist with the storytelling aspects.

When combined with materiality, lighting, and great composition, using depth of field brings a new level of sophistication to storytelling. It automatically feels like you are watching a high-quality piece just due to the fact that someone felt it was necessary to tell the story in that way, with different elements needing to command attention.

Depth of field is an expert's move that anyone can now utilize.

Typography

Text, numbers, and symbols remain a critical part of understanding business reporting, no matter how visually-oriented the information. More than likely, the most important detail you need to convey within a visualization is not the graphical elements themselves, but the text labels and explanations that bring meaning to the shapes. The textual callouts we use to highlight particular insights and findings are often the real value being delivered. Yet, high-quality type rendering is still painfully missing in most 2D, 3D, and immersive scenes. That's just not going to fly when displaying next gen business visualization.

The quality of our **typography**, or the way text is presented, is not just about its size, style, and color – but rather the combination of all those properties (and more) helping create a particular feel within our business messaging. Great typography can exude confidence, show problems, reek of formality, or create an impression of casualness.

Previously, text was often jagged, a bit blurry, or just not readable enough. This was mainly a 3D rendering and hardware problem, but now we have enough horsepower to render type very effectively within spatial scenes. The Apple Vision Pro headset delivers a notable improvement in type rendering over previous attempts. The design of their spatial computing platform takes into account the importance of high-quality typographic rendering within immersive scenes.

Composition

Any great photo, movie scene, stage play, or painting has an emphasis on the visual composition of the elements. What's the subject? Where is this? How do the individual parts relate to each other? What's the message? What does this mean to me?

Composition has everything to do with helping answer those basic questions for the viewer. Arranging individual data components spatially within a scene is only one part of composition. The relative importance of each object and any relationships between them is also conveyed by a thoughtful layout.

Positioning of the camera, or the viewer's perspective, is another aspect that can make or break achieving the desired outcome. The camera height, angle, and lens settings all help create the right feel within the composition. Getting the camera in tight to emphasize the immediacy of a situation is a clever method borrowed from cinema. Camera movement also allows the audience to follow the action over time while successive points are being made.

Great composition makes the message even stronger. The trick is to do it without anyone noticing that you're trying.

Audio

(Credit: Vizio, Inc.)

Ask anyone who makes movies for a living, and they'll likely tell you the **soundtrack** is the most underappreciated aspect of the finished product. We all love to see the star's performance, take in the amazing locations, and marvel at the computer-generated effects – but seldom do we actually notice the backing soundtrack and audio effects used to set the mood for each scene. Yes, we may happen to remember one of our favorite songs playing at a key moment, but probably not the soaring symphonic soundtrack when the hero emerges victorious. That's a real shame for the creators of those moments, but it does not diminish the importance of their work. Or the difficulty of the task.

In similar fashion, seamlessly integrating audio and effects into any type of digital presentation is a real challenge. Despite the ease of adding music, voice, or sound effects to a slide or video during editing, the job of making it seem *appropriate*, if not necessary, is one of the most difficult things in production. We are so sensitive to sound of any kind, it's gotta be right. Now add in the fact that most presentations of business information contain absolutely no audio today, and you see the magnitude of that task.

Given all that, innovative audio should be an integral part of any 4D platform we build to support this kind of cinematic experience.

Since we'll be dealing with the spatial aspects of data, we'll refer to the audio form as **Soundscapes**, versus soundtracks. They are just as sweeping or moving as in films, but more focused and tailored to the job of quickly helping to make a point or highlight a condition.

Business presentations will use cinematic quality soundscapes to direct our focus and influence impressions. They'll employ the appropriately scoped audio effects that correspond to particular states and actions of the data objects. These individual sound effects will be easily recognizable, just like sonic branding has taken centerstage in advertising and commercials.

Doing "sound design for data" will be a new vocation for those creatives with great musical instincts. This is a wide-open field filled with possibilities and many wild experiments – some of which won't work at all. We are so sensitive to sound when it's not appropriate, we immediately react negatively. But, when it's done well, like in the case of motion pictures, there's almost nothing as satisfying to behold.

(Credit: Vizio, Inc.)

Multi-Dimensionality

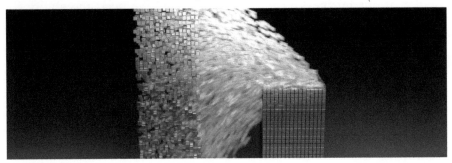

In my last book, I focused on detailing the future of communications by introducing a new construct called "Smart Information", where data inherently knows how to represent itself in multiple ways, and at different levels of detail. That functionality requires several forms to be contained within the same digital packaging, or be generated on the fly when asked for.

For instance, a book chapter like this could automatically appear as just a single summary sentence, or an infographic, or podcast audio, or a generated video, all without the author ever having to create more than the original form. The chapter appears to know how to exist in various representative forms or dimensions, each one tailored to a particular context.

We've seen this type of morphing effect during the 1990's when TV ads frequently used it to grab our attention. Having this type of dynamic format transformation (morphing) built into the data and 4D system itself delivers on the long-offered promise of personalized adaptation of content. Having the appropriate form available for the current context also helps people figure things out more effectively.

For that reason, multi-dimensionality has got to be a foundational pillar of our business visualization systems. We need the ability for any report, graph, spreadsheet, or summary, to quickly respond to current context and adapt on-the-spot to better convey meaning. Data being able to align itself at any time to the preferred way for people to consume and understand it is the superpower of 4D visual systems.

Summary

By applying a cinematic approach to business communication, we can better connect with and hold people's attention.

Trusted Simulations

Yes, take the red pill Neo

Simulation is the future of business. That's very clear. But trusting our fortunes to it, just as we would our teammates, remains the challenge.

No longer an exclusive playground for those who had access to incredibly expensive business analytics systems, business simulation engines are now routinely used to analyze potential cost reductions, support decision making, and accelerate our planning. But they don't look like what you may imagine. Today's business simulations come in many ordinary looking forms – games, spreadsheets, ChatGPT sessions, sales configurators, VR training environments, and even popular TV shows.

But, the simulations we're focused on here aren't trivial. It's not just throwing a few curveballs at next quarter's revenue forecast in Excel to see if we'd still make our numbers, it's wanting to play out what the leading financial markets are likely to do during that same revenue period. Or how we'll react to competitive threats and the effects of unforeseen supply chain challenges. This is pro-level stuff. We're not using your dad's financial modeling spreadsheets anymore.

What's been enabled through foundational Generative AI models is so far beyond what we're ordinarily thinking about, it feels like it's right out of a sci-fi movie. Any thoughts that you (or your AI copilot) have on factors that could impact the simulation's outcome can be immediately added in, adjusted throughout the session, and later used for what-if scenarios.

Literally, anything is now possible through simulation. I don't like the term "gamify" as it tends to cheapen the approach to playing what-if, but this is essentially gamifying business scenarios by allowing you to play out any number of possible timelines and end states.

Using advanced simulation techniques and technologies are the key to allowing us to fast forward time and explore new possibilities in familiar ways.

We talked about this at length in an earlier chapter, but we need to put this new capability into perspective. Being able to simulate any business scenario easily is exactly like the moment when conventional architects could begin walking around their own designs with VR headsets to feel the space without it ever needing to be built in the real world. Almost too much to believe. Yes, AI-powered simulation is that transformational.

Yet, we'll never be able to fully realize the potential of simulations if we can't fully rely on them to be **accurate**, **reliable**, and above all **trustworthy**. Despite our proclivity to trust new technologies way too early, relying on simulations to accurately plot out the path for our business is going to remain a challenge for a bit. Truth is, only fortune tellers can predict the future accurately ;-)

Getting Here

If we've finally arrived at that point in history where we're about to trust our most important business dealings to AI, we should probably take a quick look at what's got us here to boost our confidence.

Spreadsheets

Simulating business scenarios and processes is nothing new – we've had technology to help with that for quite some time. Almost from the inception of the **spreadsheet** over 40+ years ago, we've been routinely hacking together ingenious formulas and custom macros to simulate particular conditions and factors to enable financial modeling, project management, and forecasting.

Projections and forecasting are an expected part of doing business. Always have been. Hard to imagine a world where we aren't trying to figure out how expenses may add up or what would happen if revenues grew in a particular way. Spreadsheets have always been a pretty good way to simulate key aspects of business.

The problem is spreadsheets get unwieldy pretty quickly when you try to add too many formulas and variables, or they need to ingest way too much data to model a process convincingly. Add to that the human error factor, which is quite strong, and will remain so until things like Microsoft Copilot for Excel are adopted widely by business to add a level of double checks and guardrails, of sorts.

Games

If you think about it, our games are the ultimate simulators, but we don't tend to think of them that way. Despite game engines being the palette of choice for high end military or aeronautics simulations, to most of us they're just a way to relax and blow off some steam. Those same consumer-grade game engines are often the very pinnacle of technology, utilizing super advanced 3D effects to create convincing digital worlds. They use spatial sound and cinematic effects to help deliver such high levels of quality and engagement, we don't often consider how advanced the simulations truly are.

A few important aspects of game engines as simulators that we need to look more closely at:

- **Physics** – we're so used to games employing such realistic physics and lighting as a normal part of their gameplay we'd notice immediately if they didn't deliver such a high-quality experience.

- **Visuals** – every aspect of the 3D world looks stunning, from the realistic textures and materials to the real-time lighting, and certainly the detail of the digital characters.

- **Sound** – always the most overlooked part of any movie or game, expert use of spatial audio and surround sound pulls the entire experience together and delivers emotion.

- **Immersion** – few games have taken their experiences straight to VR using a headset, but you can't imagine how fun VR gaming is if you haven't tried it – you are literally in the game, and it feels like it's really happening, because it is.

All of these elements found within immersive game experiences are what we'll leverage when creating the next generation of business simulations.

Digital Twins

Fairly new onto the scene and accelerating the evolution of simulation technology, "digital twins" are highly accurate digital copies of physical places such as offices, factories, vehicles, and other types of infrastructure. These **digital twins** are often such accurate replicas of the physical world, they could pass for videos of the real places and structures they depict, not computer-generated stand-ins. Digital Twins can serve as incredibly helpful aides to so many business applications – location-based mapping, monitoring plant operations, product design, and systems engineering, just to name a few.

These digital replicas make it significantly easier to examine and analyze performance and current status of physical spaces through their use of telemetry from monitoring sensors and internal systems. By seeing the flow and movement of key elements within the systems, we also get a real sense for what's working well and what doesn't feel quite right. The direct savings that come from diagnosing design-time or real-time issues and troubleshooting problems in the field make digital twins worth the initial investment.

Focusing on the key point here – the value digital twins bring to us is their ability to accurately simulate critical parts of our businesses. This isn't a "nice to have" operational capability anymore. There's intense pressure on decision makers every day to actively manage risk while maximizing efficiency and profit in these days of post-pandemic recovery. Anything that helps provide actionable insight is deemed super impactful, and worth the cost.

Yet, those kinds of insights are so often dependent on the need to decipher cryptic reports, read dashboards, and analyze a large number of variables. We as humans cannot effectively consider all of that in any reasonable amount of time. So, we need help. And that's exactly where digital twins, AI, and advanced visualization techniques (4D) can deliver real value – by converting this from a highly manual activity to a digitally-assisted review.

Data Platforms

There's a very old expression in the computing world that couldn't be more true now than when it was first said, "Garbage in, garbage out". We have some much data at our disposal to use in these next gen business systems, but any data scientist will tell you the first step of analyzing any dataset or stream is understanding where it came from, how it was collected, and most importantly – has it been cleaned? Data collection is messy. There are all manner of bad data points from unexplainable outliers to just plain wrong values. Nevermind how it's so difficult to wrangle all of this data into a form that's usable by our analytics software. It's tough, but we have doing it.

If we are to truly make the most of data in our business simulations and historical explorations, we need to trust it. Which brings us to the need to apply a systemic approach to this daunting challenge. The industry has responded by introducing "data platforms" that are not merely standalone proprietary solutions, but rather future-leaning platforms that can federate disparate systems and data sources into one coherent pool of information that can be better utilized by anyone with access, regardless of team or region.

These modern data platforms like **Microsoft Fabric** accomplish something so critical to business that you have to wonder how we ever got along without them. They not only unify our different datasets, but allow sophisticated explorations using AI-powered analytics, aid in the governance of data across geographic and geopolitical regions, and provide easy access to people in any part of the organization. Business has been hesitant to bet on single platform solutions, so these modern platforms enable companies to keep their data secure and private while allowing approved external entities to play "behind the firewall", making audits and reporting so much easier than ever.

These modern data platforms will help to unlock an entirely new kind of business scenario – the 4D business simulation.

4D Simulations

The most significant difference between the traditional simulations we just discussed and this new era of AI-powered ones, is the seemingly magical ability to synthesize just about *anything* within our businesses by just asking for it – by anyone, anywhere, at any time. That's mind-blowing to consider given where we were just a year ago.

Made possible by the adoption of Large Language Models and Generative AI tools, these next gen simulation engines use natural language for input and refinement and have been trained on enormous amounts of existing data – business plans, models, and operational stats spanning years. They are next level in every way.

Add to that the capabilities of 4D – being able to fluidly rewind through historical data, see our present businesses in motion, and then fast forwarding to consider future forecasts, and you start to grasp the leap we are making.

The future of business will be guided by 4D simulations.

The Ultimate What-If Machine

With the widespread adoption of AI and proliferation of digital twins, seeing into the future is no longer just for fortune tellers. Now it's our turn to leverage that kind of vision and take things even further – into the realm of playing what-if with any business scenario.

Forward-looking projections have always been a key part of every business. How can we plan and execute for growth without having enough data available? It's really hard, so we do our best to look at recent trends and make our best guesses. Some of us are quite good at it, delivering fairly accurate assessments based on our experience and knowing the markets, even without using any specialized tools. Others not so fortunate.

Meanwhile, there are some who have access to quite expensive business analytics systems created specifically to do forecasting. That kind of projections-based work is a highly specialized activity, and costly, so most of us never get to see what's even possible using those systems. We just continue to do our thing manually. But now, as a direct result of the AI tsunami, that capability of doing forecasting and projecting events more accurately is coming to the mainstream and becoming part of our everyday work.

We've blown past being able to accurately predict future revenues into the realm of being able to extend those forecasts into an almost unlimited number of scenarios. By using a new type of AI-powered "4D spreadsheet" we have the ability to play what-if with just about any variable or potential situation (if enough data is available and the model was tuned properly). Better still, this is all done using natural language for input, meaning you can just have a conversation with the system to go back and forth until you have what you need to take action or at least make more informed decisions.

AI is the ultimate what-if machine.

For example, this new "what-if machine" can help you quickly assess the impact of putting electronic equipment to sleep when it's not in use to reduce the overall carbon footprint of the business. This is done of course without ever touching a physical switch by using a "digital twin" of your office and the equipment within it. That allows us calculate and assess any changes before taking on a costly or ineffective initiative in the physical world.

There are some major investments of time, effort, and learning that need to be made to fully embrace AI-based simulations like this, but it becomes pretty clear to anyone doing simulations of this kind that having your own personal what-if machine could be one of the most impactful business advancements of all time. Your simulations can run the gamut from quite simple revenue modeling all the way up to full parity digital twins of our worldwide operations. We could simulate so many parts of what we do. These could become so commonplace in our everyday jobs that in time we would **trust** them to run our businesses. Or would we?

Trust

Would we really trust an AI to do our jobs? Run our enterprises? By supercharging many of our business analytics tools and reporting with AI skills, we are rocketing toward that eventuality. If we can better predict sales, monitor operations, and do expansive scenario planning with these advanced simulations, why wouldn't we? Turns out, as always, it's a human nature thing.

It's true that walking through the impressively detailed output of all these operational simulations will raise our confidence in overall decision making. And it's also true that if we use those insights wisely, these simulations will become an integral part of the rhythm of business. All good so far. But, what makes us **nervous** about that is we are no longer the source of that key information. It's escaped our grip and appears too easy for any of our colleagues to replicate or utilize. That's a scary thought that we're no longer in control. It's also scary that we'd trust our job performance or parts of the company's operations to a machine, no matter how excellent the results are. Never mind if something goes wrong that could have been avoided if humans were in the loop.

Being the optimistic people we are, we can anticipate being able to trust these simulations over time. Afterall, there are straightforward ways to measure the effectiveness of these simulations so they can prove to us collectively we can trust their execution on monitoring, analyzing, and decision making. It will test our patience when things don't turn out as we expect, but eventually by keeping people in the loop, and using AI as a trusted partner and collaborator, we will get to the point of us being able to focus on what's truly valuable, and no longer be required to do the tedious and mundane.

These AI-powered 4D simulation systems will ultimately prove their value and accuracy over and over. They will be used widely for anything and everything. And we'll rely on and trust them to do their roles just as we do other people.

But, as any Spiderman fan knows, "with great power comes great responsibility", so we'll need to properly acknowledge and deal with some hard truths that will be revealed through simulation. This won't be easy to digest. We'll learn more than we ever wanted to know about how poorly things could go in critical areas. We will have to face some worst-case scenarios we never even considered, because the systems will outthink and outplan what people would do normally.

Simulation is a double-edged sword in that way. It brings potential futures, good and bad, into focus in unexpected ways. And perhaps that's the ultimate value of a Trusted Simulation – we actually trust it.

Summary

Trusting AI systems as we would our coworkers will take time, but ultimately we'll understand their role as copilots.

PART 4

WHAT'S NEXT?

VISUALIZING BUSINESS

Quantum Leaps

4D Systems will lead us to these breakthroughs

The invention of the spreadsheet took us all the way from using error-prone paper ledgers up to running our businesses with highly reliable digital tools. That was one of the biggest leaps forward ever in the history of business, giving us almost magical abilities to calculate complex formula-based reports on varied scenarios. But that evolution took decades to accomplish.

Now, compare that with the recent introduction of ChatGPT, Generative AI services, Copilots, and Autonomous Agents. It feels like the adoption happened almost overnight. The speed at which we are innovating with AI has never been seen before in the modern era – it's shocking, and a lost cause to continually track. But that's not the part we should be paying attention to.

All of this innovation has created the perfect storm of opportunity. We are living in an age of accelerated creativity and accomplishment. Impossible is nothing, indeed.

Time Machines

Humanity has always yearned to travel back and forth in time. Some of our most exciting and I dare say riveting stories are based on that premise. Adventurers exploring historical periods or even leaping into the great unknown of the future are two of the most interesting things we could ever hope for. Time travel appears to be an important part of our internal programming. It never fails to stimulate our imaginations with limitless possibilities.

Careful what you wish for.

The 4D visualization and simulation systems described in this book are just the beginning. Yes, they allow us to easily scrub back and forth through historical corporate data, and most allow for future forecasting and prediction based on current execution and trends. That's transformational already, true. But that's nothing compared to what's about to happen. We are about to achieve the creation of digital time machines.

By leveraging Generative AI to synthesize what we may not have access to already, we can literally experience anything, anywhere, at any time, for any reason. Think about that for a second.

Time travel has truly profound implications for education, culture, business, and ultimately the evolution of humanity. Yes, you're right we're not going to be strapping Jodie Foster into a futuristic time sphere like in *Contact* anytime soon, but we are going to have digital facsimiles of that. Let's just hope the Morlocks are not waiting for us. All that danger aside, let's talk about how and why this is happening.

Two very different Time Machines, but both transport us

Our 4D business systems will directly lead to the development of general-purpose digital time machines. Why? Because they operate on all the same principles. And as perpetually curious tinkerers, we won't be able to help ourselves. It's all so straightforward to the engineering brain – Data fuels the historical aspects, and synthesized data can be subbed in when it doesn't exist. Spatial Computing technologies generate the convincing, immersive environments dynamically. AI provides the natural language interface and what-if capabilities. Web3 tech helps preserve privacy and makes these experiences monetizable by their creators via cryptocurrencies. And advanced visualization techniques aid in the narrative and storytelling aspects. All combined expertly within a magical experience.

These digital time machines will allow you to ask for any situation to be illustrated in some way, past or present, historical or future. The system will know your context and display it in the most appropriate medium for you personally, and you'll be able to pause, rewind, and fast forward fluidly from within any segment. Not enough? How about being able to change any part of it, at any time, to see the impact.

No one can imagine where time machines will take us when they're available to all of us. The highly dynamic and exciting nature of exploring newly created moments in time will in itself be enough to keep us coming back. And imagine if it becomes just another tool for us to use at work, home, or school, completely meshed with our regular responsibilities.

Time Machines are finally here.

Information Spaces

One of the enduring memes in science fiction movies has always been going "inside" the computer to fly through fantastical landscapes of colorful light, impressive looking chip sets, security structures, and network connections. The inside of a computer system is a wonderland of unexplored digital realms. One of those spaces is usually dedicated to showing documents and schematics of the building floorplans to support the movie's plotline. But, in all seriousness, the notion of being immersed within a computer system is a recurring favorite in many films for good reason – it's thrilling to consider. And it's about to get real.

Information Spaces are not a bunch of digital documents hanging in mid-air. That's ridiculous. And completely useless. These 4D spaces are a new construct and paradigm for exploring information. By extracting and isolating content from documents, then breaking it free from its former digital container, we enable an entirely new kind of experience. When displaying content in a "pure form" (meaning it's best representation for the current context), arranged within a spatial setting, it sets up an interaction model that couldn't be more natural because it's based on the properties and expectations of the physical world, but made better by being digitally authentic.

For example, imagine this book is rendered in an Information Space. What you'd see is not a bunch of floating pages of text, but rather an elegant looking sea of type, some of which is closer and in focus, the rest clearly in some types of an ordered structure. Gesturing or conversing with the AI yields shifts in the ordering and look of the information itself, bringing the most relevant content or correct answer to the foreground. Related and relevant content is connected, and always available, but not taking your focus unless asked for or needed for the current task and flow.

"Information Landscapes" by the legendary Muriel Cooper of MIT (1994)
(Credit: Muriel Cooper (c) MIT Media Lab. July 1994)

What we've become accustomed to as individual web pages will transform over time to being more expansive information spaces, with documents and files themselves being deconstructed and flowed into more appropriate forms and shapes for immersive work. Infused with

AI via Copilots and background tasks, the feel of working within Information Spaces is more like *Minority Report* than what you'd expect from a web page.

The Neuroverse

Emotion is one of the missing elements of modern digital experiences. Knowing what people are actually feeling when immersed in various digital experiences is a big gap in our overall understanding of online social behavior. Partially a product of the technologies we had to work with, and partially our decision for interfaces and tools to be neutral and objective, we've spent the better part of thirty years designing experiences that don't wade very far into the emotional side of things.

Yes, it's true that social media can evoke highly charged emotional responses, but that's a byproduct and (perhaps) not a design goal. We have purposely stayed out of the emotional side of product and service design. Until now.

The **Neuroverse** is a digital substrate or layer that's a collection of biometric data from sensors, cameras, microphones, and wearables that have captured your emotional state and reactions over time, or in real-time. We'll use it to surface emotions and feelings to higher-level layers of the online experience, such as the Web, Mobile, Cloud, Spatial Computing, and of course business visualizations.

At its heart, the Neuroverse is a service layer that provides key input to the AI models being used to run experiences and whatever type of user interface is being presented to us – whether that's voice, text, screen-based, or projection. Just as databases and AI models are used to provide the data utilized in our services, the Neuroverse will provide the emotional aspects of the people currently active.

The way we interact within services will be greatly enhanced by employing a layer of emotional understanding or EQ, much like the way people can sense what's happening in face-to-face situations. We know the social norms and psychology of many situations that our current tools know nothing of. That's why as designers we always lament the need for people to adapt to the system vs. the other way around.

We will finally be able to visualize emotion and feelings
(Credit: Inga Popesko, "Wired up" The Neruo Bureau 2014)

The Neuroverse helps give digital systems secure access to this layer of insights into the emotional state of people. By combining various inputs such as micro-expressions, voice cues, heart and pulse rates, temperature, and motion, the system can weigh its responses and queries to fit the situation more appropriately.

Injecting emotion and feelings into our everyday interactions with digital systems is as logical as it is overdue. We have gone on far too long without having this vital part of interacting with humanity in our digital lives.

Quantum Visualization

Much has been made of the world-changing advances that quantum computing could bring. By utilizing a completely different approach to computer architecture and programming based on quantum physics, quantum computing holds the promise of unlocking processing speeds and attacking problem domains that are almost unimaginable today.

That said, numerous hurdles must be surmounted before practical, large-scale quantum computers become a reality. Many scientists and engineers are working towards the development of dependable qubits and the enhancement of stability and control in quantum systems, with the ultimate aim of unlocking the full potential of this mind-boggling technology.

Tomorrow's quantum computers have the potential to perform calculations at a speed that surpasses today's classical computers by ridiculous orders of magnitude, paving the way for solving previously unapproachable problems across a wide range of disciplines including climate forecasting, cryptography, optimization, drug discovery, and environmental science.

Quantum Visualization accelerates the possibilities

Another quantum leap for visualizing business is on the horizon. When they finally come online, quantum computers will completely redefine our expectations of what's achievable when it comes to modeling and visualizing the most intricate and complex aspects of our businesses. Being able to conceive of a business idea, build it, launch it, analyze its effect on markets and consumers, then see its projected evolution over years could be done in less than a minute someday. The possibilities are endless.

See you there.

The Future's Past

by David Brunner

For most "knowledge workers", the daily grind of emails, chats, task management apps, spreadsheets, and slide presentations feels almost exactly like it did decades ago. Even for those of us who work at the cutting edge of technology with AI, it still seems impossibly distant to the realization of Mike's futuristic, multi-dimensional, immersive datascapes. Yet, that world of 4D business systems is surely closer than we think, because as he points out, such a profoundly natural and intuitive way to work will find a way to spring into existence. And in fact, his vision for wide deployment of 4D business systems has deep parallels to another foundational transformation of work that took place in the second half of the 20th century for manufacturing.

The ability for Japanese automobile companies to rapidly grow from their humble beginnings to achieve shockingly high levels of efficiency and quality that far exceeded the capabilities of their American competitors is the stuff of legend in the business world. When I was a doctoral student at the Harvard Business School, the faculty often talked about "lean manufacturing" and the Toyota Production System. The processes and innovative technologies developed for managing these incredibly complex manufacturing operations forever changed the way we approached that work.

One of the key tenets of these innovative systems was *mieru-ka* (見える化), a Japanese neologism that translates into "making visible" or "visualization". Some of the most obvious examples of mieru-ka in a factory are indicator lights showing current status, distinctive sounds emitted by robots on the move, and markings on the floor or shelves that show where parts or equipment should be placed.

Making the structure of manufacturing activity visible to workers supports a second key feature of the Toyota production system: *kaizen* (改善), often translated as "continuous improvement." The designers of these systems believe kaizen occurs through experimentation, learning, and innovation. Rather than isolating the innovation function in R&D labs separate from actual operations, the system emphasizes the importance of all workers participating in the discovery of new and better ways of working to continuously improve.

Even if you've never toured a Japanese automobile factory, after reading this book you may be able to imagine how a digital twin of such a factory could make information flows and business decision-making more tangible and intuitive. Perhaps some of the massive queue of customer support tickets backing up are brighter colors because of their severity, or flashing and emitting worrisome noises because they have not been handled promptly, or because they were received from particularly important stakeholders. Maybe one of the team areas of those who are handling the requests has turned red because their workload needs to be re-balanced.

These kinds of problems happen in our businesses every day, but instead of being visible and obvious, they are (at best) surfaced on analytics "dashboards" that are too often out of sight, out of mind. When these problems are visualized with rich sensory cues, patterns jump out and people can spot opportunities for intervention, experimentation, and improvement. Not to mention the huge difference seeing situations earlier in time or projected out would bring to management.

In hindsight, it's remarkable how long it took for manufacturing companies to recognize the benefits of *mieru-ka* and *kaizen*. Looking back a few decades further, the benefits of interchangeable parts and assembly lines were just as transformative at the time. Such is the nature of paradigm shifts: they become obvious only after the fact. In the domain of knowledge work, it's remarkable that our organizations function as effectively as they do given the lack of operational transparency and business process visualization.

Indeed, so many decisions, processes, bottlenecks, erroneous calculations, data inconsistencies, and all manner of waste are shrouded in obscurity, because there's simply no way to visualize all the different parts of the business and how they interconnect. In fact, much of Toyota's success came simply from obsessively reducing waste in every step of every manufacturing process, thereby radically increasing productivity and quality. Yet while Toyota succeeded magnificently back then on the physical factory floor, 20th-century methods cannot bring 360-degree, real-time visibility to the abstract, informational operations of business that determine productivity and performance in 21st-century organizations.

By projecting information flows into human-centered, multi-dimensional spaces that enable and encourage virtual exploration and experimentation, the methods detailed in *Visualizing Business* will unlock large and lucrative opportunities for nearly every complex enterprise. Quite significantly, Mike emphasizes that visualization is not about simplification. It's true that modularity and well-designed business architecture can reduce complexity, but only to a point. Mike gives the brilliant example of a prime number, that just cannot be factored any further, "it is what it is." Similarly, our businesses are inherently complex, epitomized by the enormous global automobile industry with its extremely intricate supply chains and exceedingly precise temporal and spatial choreography. 4D visualization and simulation will help us grasp the essential characteristics of complex business systems in the same way those auto makers used the physical design of the factory to bring clarity to the complexity of automobile manufacturing.

Another crucial component of *Visualizing Business* is Artificial Intelligence. And again, there's a powerful analog to physical manufacturing found in the rise of AI. In both instances, by automating the more routine and taxing aspects of the work, humans can be liberated to focus on more creative tasks. That was true in manufacturing, and is now at the heart of many observations about using AI. Yet, there is a key difference. Although we can create digital twins of the real-world factories and their operations, they do not have access to the kind of time travel and simulation that Mike describes here. That's only possible in the virtual world of 4D datascapes, which in turn brings with it the potential for limitless exploration of what-if scenarios. By using a 4D approach to enable what was prohibitively difficult and costly, we can kick off the same type of transformative business advantage that mieru-ka and kaizen brought.

And finally, a key aspect of 4D that Mike touched on was the way that time travel and simulation are force multipliers for human learning and understanding. The more our businesses become instrumented and augmented by AI, the greater the return we can expect on our investments in people. We will more easily, and deeply, understand and see emerging opportunities that align with our visions and aspirations. We'll more quickly build action plans to reach our goals. And ultimately, by working within these deeply immersive, multidimensional, multi-sensory datascapes, we will create far more value for our customers and stakeholders than we could ever hope to achieve in our current knowledge work paradigm.

It was only after manufacturing fell into a bleak malaise in the last century that researchers turned their attention to the roots of superior productivity, and even then the new paradigms for manufacturing took decades to diffuse globally. Fortunately, business leaders now know that they cannot afford to ignore emerging technologies, and Mike Pell has shown us the way to embrace the future by *Visualizing Business*.

David Brunner
Silicon Valley
July 2023

David Brunner is the founder and CEO of ModuleQ, a cutting-edge AI-powered insights company, based in Silicon Valley.

CLOSING THOUGHTS

Deceptively powerful and stunningly beautiful, 4D is a monumental leap forward in conveying business information effectively that has always been right there in front of us, hiding in plain sight, waiting to be unlocked. All it took was the convergence of human ingenuity, Artificial Intelligence, and the rise of a medium capable of magic.

And while we can't know exactly where all these new capabilities will ultimately take us, we do know that despite all our technological advancements, people will always be the most important part of the equation. Aways.

It's up to all of us now.
Let's do this.

Until next time

M. Pell

ACKNOWLEDGEMENTS

Dave Brown
Microsoft Research

A very special thanks to Dave Brown, who has inspired me for close to a decade with his groundbreaking work on 3D data visualization. He is truly an innovator in this field and an exceptionally gifted technical artist. In fact, many of the illustrations in this book are based on his previously published research at MSR. Couldn't have conveyed my points anywhere as well without your stellar work. Thank you Dave!

Microsoft Corporation
Redmond, WA

Thank you for consistently supporting the idea that we all grow by sharing what we've learned to make each other better. My deepest respect to all of my colleagues and friends who push to improve the world around us for everyone, every day.

Family, Friends, and Colleagues
Worldwide

Again, there are way too many special people for me to thank properly for their inspiration, dedication, and friendship. You all know exactly who you are, and how much I truly appreciate you.

ABOUT THE AUTHOR

M. Pell

Bold, insightful, and uncompromising, M. Pell is widely recognized as a world-class designer and inspiring thought leader.

Pell's first book "Envisioning Holograms" is considered a must-have for tomorrow's most influential storytellers and explorers. His futuristic look forward "The Age of Smart Information" details how the fundamental nature of information is changing due to AI and Spatial Computing. This book "Visualizing Business" arrives just as the world is recognizing the power of combining AI and Data.

Pell has been on the leading edge of design and innovation throughout his entire career in the tech industry. Highlights include inventing Adobe Acrobat and PDF, the stylized Font menu, created groundbreaking 3D type tools for Pixar RenderMan, pioneered the first Metaverse in the 90's, and recently leading The Microsoft Garage in New York City – the company's worldwide program for innovation.

Learn more at Mike-Pell.com

MENTIONS

Some of the people, companies, and products mentioned here:

ARHT Media	arht.tech
Apple, Inc.	apple.com
Boston Dynamics	bostondynamics.com
Dolby	dolby.com
Flow Immersive	flowimmersive.com
LAMINA1	lamina1.com
Leia, Inc.	leiainc.com
Microsoft Corporation	microsoft.com
ModuleQ	moduleq.com
NVIDIA	nvidia.com
OpenAI	openai.com
Refik Anadol	refikanadol.com
Unity	unity3d.com
Unreal	unrealengine.com
Vizio	vizio.com

UPDATES

You have my sincere thanks for reading this book. Please follow me for bonus content and new posts. I'd also really appreciate you sharing your thoughts about this book with friends.

BOOK SITE
for all the latest news, updates, and examples:

https://VisualizingBusiness.com

SOCIAL
Please connect or follow me in any of these ways:

 https://LinkedIn.com/in/mikepell

 https://Mike-Pell.com

 https://x.com/_MPelll_

 https://Instagram.com/mpell_nyc

AUTHOR SITE

Mike-Pell.com

PREVIOUS BOOKS

Thanks for finishing this book! If you are interested in reading or sharing more by M. Pell, you can find the other books here:

The Age of Smart Information (2019)
by M. Pell

How AI and Spatial Computing are transforming business communications.

https://TheAgeOfSmartInformation.com

Envisioning Holograms (2017)
by M. Pell

A textbook for designing breakthrough experiences using Spatial Computing

https://EnvisioningHolograms.com

INSPIRATION

One of my favorite quotes ever.

SKETCHES

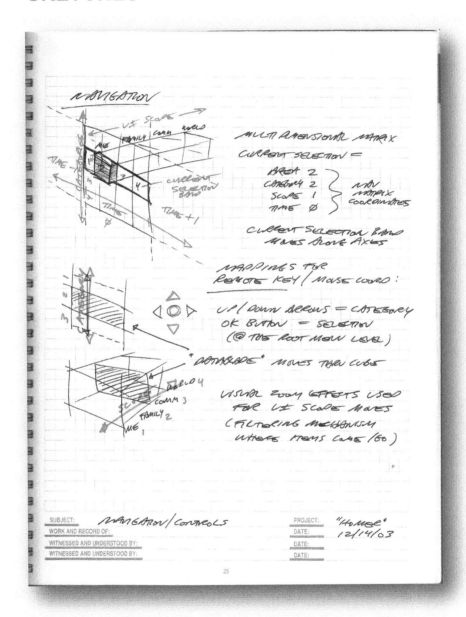

This is where the idea for the 4D Time Machine started back in 2003 when I started sketching out how we'd interact with it.

SKETCHES

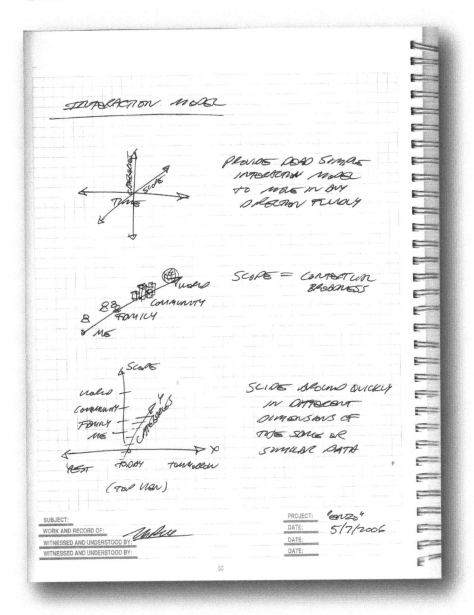

I needed to work out the core interaction model before I could get to the detailed parts of the design. Still holds up well today.

SKETCHES

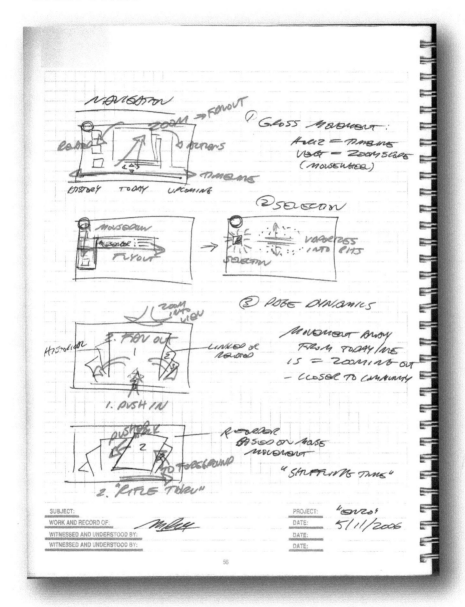

In these studies, interacting with a screen via gestures and touch is equivalent to being immersed in a spatial environment.

SKETCHES

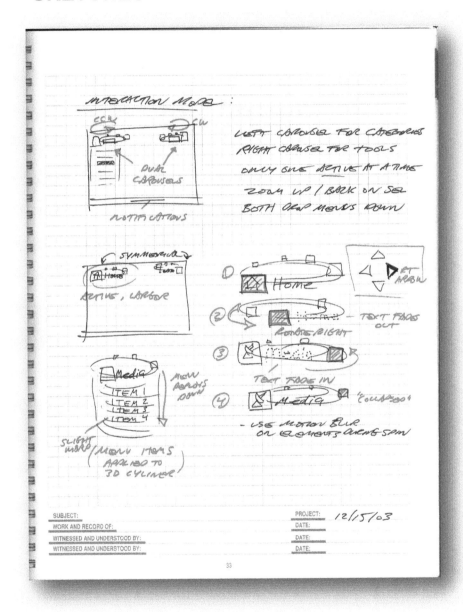

Time figures into these interface explorations around easy access to content from various sources.

SKETCHES

This was one of my earliest sketches of using time within financial data. Note the use of near real-time analysis and reporting.

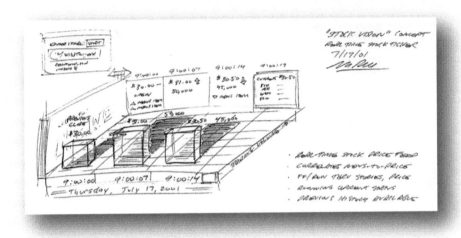

And the use of the "datablade" to shuttle back and forth through time...

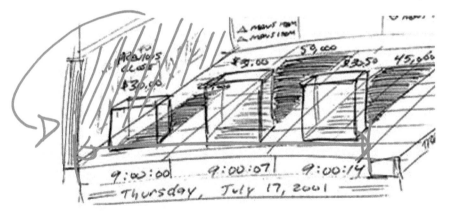

NOTES

NOTES

NOTES

Printed in the USA
CPSIA information can be obtained
at www.ICGtesting.com
LVHW052153131023
760911LV00031B/347/J